In Light of Yesterday

The Backstory of the Global Economy

BRADY RAANES, CFA, CFP®, CMT

ISBN 13: 978-1-7332305-2-0

TABLE OF CONTENTS

ACKNOWLEDGEMENTS

This book would not be possible (or at least, not as good) without the loving support of several people. First, to my wife, Christen, thank you for allowing me time over the previous two and a half years to write and research on nights and weekends. Your patience and continued support have been inspirational. You helped make the book more approachable and entertaining, and I am very grateful for you. I couldn't ask for a better life partner!

To my mother, JoAnn, you have always been a fantastic sounding board, editor, idea generator, researcher, and cheerleader. I can't thank you enough for the countless hours you've spent reading my many rough drafts and talking through the stories to make this book possible. Also, thanks for raising me.

To my father and business partner, Duane, thank you for bringing me into the fascinating and challenging world of investments. Throughout the years, you've challenged me to improve myself, and allowed me to pursue my passions. We've had an amazing working relationship for nearly twenty years, and I'm so appreciative of your insight, honesty, and guidance through the years.

To my boys, Manny and Beni, thanks for patiently cheering me on while simultaneously forgiving me for spending my Saturday mornings hunched over the computer. I hope my dedication to research and self-improvement will be motivational to you both later in life. Whatever you choose to do, try to do it well. Find something you are passionate about, and separate yourself from others with your dedication and hard work.

A special thanks to my coworkers Duane Raanes, Kent Oliver, Jim Grenn, and Kelsey Addison for all your feedback on titles and covers, and for all your hard work with the sister podcast for this book, *Domino*. You guys are truly fun to work with, and I greatly appreciate your friendship and loving support. Also, Jim wants it to be known that he helped choose the final title. Personally, I liked *Deja Poo: We've Seen This Crap Before*, but whatever.

To my friend Bill Schoell, thank you so much for reading my rough drafts, providing insights, and cheering me on along the way. Your cheap wine is always appreciated. I'm truly humbled to consider you a friend.

To my clients, your trust and confidence have persisted throughout market cycles. You are truly the motivation for my efforts and the reason I strive to better understand the economy and the world around us.

To Raymond James Financial Services, thank you for letting financial advisors pursue their passion. I've worked for other firms, and I can truly say that Raymond James takes the cake as the friendliest firm on the street. Many investment firms would prohibit advisors from writing books, producing podcasts, or making videos. Thank you for the flexibility and freedom you provide!

To my editor, Harry David, thank you for the feedback and the idea to reorganize the book. Your edits were timely, accurate, and incredibly helpful. I look forward to working with you again. Also, a special shout out to Nick Ortego with Ortego Creative… thanks for all the work on the audiobook!

To my in-laws, Reggie and Denise Palmer, you had nothing to do with the book, but you're great people. Plus, you let me marry your daughter… and I greatly appreciate that!

To my other friends, who also had nothing to do with the book, I'll list your names here as a test to see if you actually read this book. If you see your name, shoot me a text (in no particular order): Josh and Lauren Etheridge, Justin and Jenny Green, Brent and Mary Barham, Josh and Kara Barham, Brad and Jenny Boudreaux, Jason and Melanie Lindsey, Seth and Shasta Miles, Tommy and Alicia Teepell, Chad and Carmen Davis, Kent and Candace Oliver, Rick and Vanessa Raanes, KK and Malorie Aldridge, Warren and Jessi Flynt, Virgil and Mary Palmer, Josh and Courtney Speed, Steven and Raquel Wood, Paul and Lindsey Mickle, Will and Lee Herrin, Whitney and Paxton Dickson, Julie Anna and Jason Perry, Erin and Larry Pacific, Steve and Alecia Wood, Holly and Bobby Shirley, Jake Ford, Chris and Amy Martin, Quincy DeJarnett, Ben and Alisa Berteau, Jon and Sara

Schock, Forrest and Marie Hartel, Ashley and Brittany Read, and Sharron and Terry Bellew.

Most importantly, to the reader, thank you for choosing to go on this journey with me. It's my hope that you walk away from this book with a better understanding of the economy, some fun stories to share at cocktail parties, and a little insight into what the future may hold.

INTRO

Edward Lorenz was out of coffee. He entered the final numbers into his computer and pushed the button to begin the simulation before leaving his office to get a refill.

Lorenz's computer-simulated weather-pattern project had taken a substantial portion of his time since he secured his position as a professor at MIT. About an hour passed before Lorenz returned to examine the results from the program's two-month weather simulation. Computers ran slowly in 1961. Lorenz was stunned at the outputs; the results differed dramatically from his previous readings. He had run a short-term weather simulation earlier, but he had wanted to repeat the exercise to examine a longer time. He immediately suspected computer trouble.

"Before calling for service I decided to see just where the mistake had occurred," Lorenz recalled. Lorenz had taken a seemingly small short-cut when entering the most recent data. The computer stored numbers to an accuracy of six decimal places, but the printout of results from the first simulation rounded the numbers to only three decimal places. When typing in the new weather conditions, Lorenz had entered the rounded-off numbers. For example, Lorenz entered 0.506 rather than 0.506127. Lorenz had served as a meteorologist for the US Army during World War II. He didn't have a formal degree in meteorology, but he was well versed in mathematics, having earned degrees at both Dartmouth and Harvard. Lorenz believed he could apply much of the mathematics he already knew to meteorology to get a more accurate forecast. This time, however, his numbers seemed outrageous.

"I found that the new values at first repeated the old ones, but soon afterward differed by one and then several units in the last decimal place, and then began to differ in the next to the last place and then in the place before that. In fact, the differences more or less steadily doubled in size every four days or so, until all resemblance with the original output disappeared somewhere in the second month."

The output led Lorenz to a powerful conclusion: incredibly small changes can lead to exponentially large consequences when dealing with complex systems. Lorenz found it virtually impossible to predict a long-term meteorological outcome with much accuracy because of the weather system's complexity. This observation serves as a basis for what we now refer to as chaos theory, a field of study dealing with the effect of small changes in complex systems. The term *chaos theory* does not imply chaotic outcomes in the sense of mass hysteria. It merely implies that outcomes move from a linear, deterministic relationship into the realm of unpredictable outcomes. Lorenz's insights apply not just to meteorology, but to virtually every field dealing with complex systems. The term *complex system* is broad and speaks specifically to a field of research that studies systems with feedback loops, adaptive learning, and nonlinear relationships. The global economy is a prime example.

In 1972, Lorenz presented his research at the American Association for the Advancement of Science with the title "Does the Flap of a Butterfly's Wings in Brazil Set Off a Tornado in Texas?" The imagery was a hit, and Lorenz's theory became known as the butterfly effect.

The butterfly effect described by Lorenz reflects the belief that forecasting the outcome of events in complex systems is nearly impossible. As we will see, his theory also holds important truths for the world of economics. Trillions of factors are at play in the modern economy. Small changes in interest rates, currency values, or banking regulations can have huge impacts on the global economy. Changing any variable runs the risk of creating feedback loops, such as manias that create asset bubbles and wreak havoc on capital markets. The global economy is a unique example of a man-made complex system, with each country maintaining a unique economic balance that can be disrupted by the smallest of changes. The future impact of a change is unknowable at the time; however, by studying similar instances from the past we may be able to glean insight into the impact of similar changes in the future.

An important question arose during the depths of the Great Depression: how does one measure the performance of an economy? No one seemed to know, including the group of experts called by the Hoover administration to testify at a congressional hearing in 1932.

Up until that point, policy makers gauging the health of the economy had relied on limited and arbitrary data such as stock indices' performance, freight-car loadings, and industrial production. This patchwork of information was all they had, and it formed the basis for the policy decisions surrounding the Great Depression. Comprehensive data on national income and economic output simply didn't exist. Shortly after the congressional hearings, the Senate asked the Commerce Department for help. The Commerce Department agreed to commission a study to develop a uniform way of tracking the strength of the economy.

Simon Kuznets was in charge of the assignment. Kuznets was sharp. He had received a PhD from Columbia, where he had done extensive research on the relationship between pricing and production. Kuznets was assigned a small team to help with the research. It took nearly five years before he and his team had a report to present to Congress, but the research was groundbreaking.

The team's work was meticulous as they had researched nearly every output and input for which there was sufficient data. Kuznets kept detailed records of each variable to determine its importance. Ultimately, the report became the prototype for what we now refer to as gross domestic product (GDP), a comprehensive measure of economic activity. For the first time, economists had a truly tangible way of tracking the performance of the economy. Politicians had a measuring stick they could use to judge the economic impact of a policy change. As a result, the growth rate of GDP became a national obsession as it quickly became the scorecard for the country. With a deeper understanding of the economy, policy makers were free to attempt to manipulate the business cycle.

"If you want to know why GDP matters, you can just put yourself back in the 1930 period, where we had no idea what was happening to our economy," said William Nordhaus, a Yale economist. "There were people then who said things were fine and others who said things weren't fine. But we had no comprehensive measures, so we looked at things like boxcar loadings."

With the success of the new benchmark, the economic profession grew in stature. Economists quickly became a guiding light on most policy matters; their expert opinions were held in the highest regard. Policy makers came to view economic growth as the primary driver for most decisions. Few stopped to question whether GDP should be the benchmark.

GDP measures activity in the economy, but not necessarily the usefulness of the activity. Is economic activity good for society? Not always. As we will explore in greater detail with an examination of modern-day China, not all of the inputs to gross domestic product have societal benefit. Building useless roads and bridges or ghost cities can add to economic activity, but it is of little value.

Natural disasters such as hurricanes typically add to economic growth because of rebuilding efforts, but the net economic effect of rebuilding is typically zero. In 2010, the British Petroleum oil-rig explosion took the lives of eleven workers and leaked three million barrels of oil into the Gulf of Mexico, but it actually increased GDP because of the cleanup costs. Likewise, if a country were to ravage and sell its natural resources, GDP would increase, but the country would be left without long-term viability.

"The pursuit of growth can be quite dangerous," said Peter Victor, an economist at York University in Toronto.

The obsession with GDP growth also occasionally leads policy makers to make detrimental decisions in the name of short-term economic activity such as nixing tax hikes during an economic boom or overstimulating a healthy economy with money printing and interest rate cuts.

Still, GDP growth remains the prime measure for an economy's success, and increasing GDP remains the goal for most economists and politicians. There is nothing inherently wrong with using the measure to gauge the health of an economy. Improving GDP numbers typically suggest that economic activity is strong, which is especially useful in measuring the recovery after an economic calamity, but blind pursuit of GDP growth can frequently lead to policy error and misallocation of resources.

This book will explore the pursuit of economic growth for five key regions: Latin America, Europe, Japan, China, and the United States. For simplicity, I've combined all the countries of Latin America into one section and the European countries into another. Each region took a dramatically different approach in its attempt to create economic growth, with varying degrees of success.

Latin America has struggled more than comparable regions, partially because politicians bet heavily on the price of natural resources such as oil. Unfortunately for the region, the focus on commodities led to misplaced investment and overleverage, ultimately resulting in economic calamity, malnourishment, immigration, and a booming illegal-drug industry.

Following the two world wars, European countries, trying to preserve peace in the region, created a strange patchwork economy sewn together with a common currency, lax regulation, and nonuniform tax collection.

As for Japan, the country sustained consistent economic growth for decades while emerging as a leader in technological innovation, but poor central bank policies and lax banking regulation created a real estate bubble. Just as Japan appeared poised to surpass the US, the unicorn died. The country has been battling deflation and an aging population base ever since.

China's approach to economic growth is perhaps the most distinctive. The story of its economic ascension begins in 1978 with the establishment of special economic zones, which opened it up to foreign investment and trade. The next three decades culminated in the largest rise in economic activity the world has ever seen. Since 2008, however, the obsession with economic growth appears to have fueled an unsustainable real estate bubble and amassed a mountain of debt.

When I began my investment-services career at age twenty-two, I lacked a practical knowledge of the workings of our global economy and the context that can be gleaned from stories of the past. My desire to better understand historical economic relationships led me down various paths of research. I developed a fascination with the "butterfly-wing flapping" events that shaped our global economy.

This book is not an academic endeavor written for an audience of economists, but rather a broad look at compelling events that have occurred throughout the world over the past five decades, culminated in concerning levels of risk-taking and debt. The lead-up to the present day encompasses stories of greed and fear, naivety and shrewdness, and good intentions with unintended consequences. I hope the reader will be enlightened, educated, and better equipped to respond to the ups and downs of both domestic and global economic changes. Hopefully, gaining an understanding of the stories that shaped our current economy will enable the reader to better answer an important question: What can we do today, in light of yesterday, to prepare for tomorrow?

PART 1

The United States

1

THE END OF THE GOLD STANDARD

The time has come for a new economic policy for the United States.

— *Richard Nixon*

Catoctin Park is located in North Central Maryland, about sixty miles northwest of Washington, DC. With twenty-five miles of trails through hardwood forests and panoramic views of the Monocacy Valley, the park attracts a steady flow of city dwellers wishing to get away from the hustle and bustle of life in the city. Hikers and campers frequent the scenic lookouts on weekends.

Nestled within the cozy six-thousand-acre park is a small "Closed to the public" sign at the turn-off to a narrow road, which leads to a well-fortified, two-hundred-acre compound known as Camp David. Completely hidden from public view, Camp David has served as a retreat for thirteen presidents since the early 1940s, starting with Franklin D. Roosevelt. The area, originally dubbed Shangri-La by Roosevelt, was closed to the public for exclusive presidential use. The compound has since been modernized: equipped with a swimming pool, bowling alley, skeet-shooting range, helicopter pad, and eleven separate cabins. Inside the presidential cabin, Aspen

Lodge, is an elevator that descends two hundred feet to a secret underground complex housing a communications center, a war room, and more sleeping accommodations in case of national emergency. Over the decades, American presidents have used Camp David to relax with their families and friends, convene with advisors, and host foreign heads of state.

President Nixon chose Camp David as the site for a secret emergency meeting in mid August 1971. He and fifteen of his closest advisors arrived by helicopter and disappeared into a cabin to begin a discussion that would last the entire weekend. Two days earlier, the United Kingdom had requested a conversion of $3 billion into gold. Similar requests had been made by different countries over the previous few decades, but this request was larger than usual. The United Kingdom was within its rights to make the request as dollars were convertible into gold at a fixed price of thirty-five dollars an ounce. But handing over $3 billion worth of gold would have depleted roughly a quarter of the United State's total supply. Nixon and his advisors had difficult decisions to make.

The group that accompanied the president to Camp David consisted of his most trusted inner circle of advisors and one fairly unknown economist: Paul Volcker. Volcker was one of the few attendees with any background in economic matters. Despite being the youngest in attendance, forty-three-year-old Volcker was seen as the technical expert and the main proponent of the emergency meeting. Though largely unknown by Nixon, Volcker was well qualified. He was a Princeton graduate with a master's in political economy from Harvard. Volcker had also attended the London School of Economics and served as a Federal Reserve Bank economist, a Chase Manhattan Bank economist, the Treasury Department's director of financial analysis, and finally undersecretary for monetary affairs at the Treasury.

Volcker was hard to overlook: he stood 6'7" and frequently smoked Cuban cigars. His unusual height had even kept him out of the military when he attempted to join, as it considered any height above 6'6" a physical impairment. When playing basketball also hadn't panned out, Volcker had turned to a life as a public servant. Nixon knew Volcker by name based on the briefings Volcker had frequently prepared for him. But beyond that, any level of trust Volcker enjoyed with the president had been imputed to him by his boss, Treasury Secretary John Connally.

Connally had been appointed to his position only seven months earlier—handpicked by Nixon, who viewed him as potentially a future political superstar and presidential candidate. Connally is perhaps most remembered for the time he served as Texas governor, from 1963 until 1969. He had been seriously wounded while riding in President Kennedy's car in Dallas at the time of Kennedy's assassination on November 22, 1963. Fragments of the bullet that killed Kennedy remained lodged in Connally's thigh and wrist.

In the short time since his arrival at the Treasury, Connally had come to rely heavily on Paul Volcker's thorough research and analysis to bring him up to speed on economic matters. The two made for an amusing pair. Connally was boisterous and made it clear where he stood on any given topic, playing the role of an outspoken Texan to a tee. Volcker's introverted personality paled in comparison to Connally's John Wayne style. As a polished political machine, Connally had a unique ability to put a political spin on almost anything, while Volcker stuck to the facts and carefully added disclaimers to each opinion.

Volcker's main concern at the time of the emergency meeting centered on the imbalance between the gold supply in the United States and the dollars held overseas by foreign governments, which could be converted to gold at any time. The imbalance between the two was dramatic. Seventy billion dollars were held as foreign reserves outside the United States. Correspondingly, based on the convertibility option, the United States needed $70 billion worth of gold on hand to honor any conversion requests. The US gold reserves, however, were woefully low at about $12 billion. Based on the $35/oz. price at which gold was convertible in 1971, the United States was about forty-seven thousand tons short of what it needed to balance the scale. That sum would have equated to more than half of the gold ever mined in the history of the world at the time. For reference, central banks combined have less than forty thousand tons of total reserves today.

The imbalance was unsustainable, but that was largely unknown to the rest of the world. The truth, however, could quickly be exposed with large conversion requests. The United Kingdom's request to convert $3 billion was cause enough for concern. Nixon had no desire to hand over a quarter of the government's total gold supply, but he feared that rejecting the UK's request could send a frightening signal to the rest of the world about the value of the dollar.

Volcker had been vocal about the impending dilemma for the last two years, preparing and distributing research papers on a regular basis. The administration had taken a wait-and-see approach in hopes that time would heal the problem. It hadn't.

Gold has long been an important element in the US economy. As a precious metal known for its resistance to corrosion and viewed as a dependable store of value, gold has been used for coinage and jewelry throughout recorded history. The search for gold was even one of the driving factors in Europe's exploration and colonization of the American continents.

By the mid-nineteenth century, most countries backed their paper currencies with physical gold. Gold, however, was cumbersome for large transactions, but paper currencies backed by physical gold offered a method to standardize transactions in the booming world trade. As long as convertibility remained intact, paper currency would have a guaranteed value tied to something real.

Convertibility to gold implied a high level of trust in the government. Many European countries suspended the gold standard during World War I in order to print enough money to pay for military involvement, inadvertently creating hyperinflation in many countries. Several eventually returned to a gold standard following the war.

Prior to the Great Depression, physical gold backed all US dollars in circulation. Dollars could be exchanged for gold at a fixed rate of $20.67 per ounce with the Federal Reserve. When the stock market crashed in 1929, investors clamored for physical gold. As banks failed, people began to hoard gold given their growing distrust of financial institutions. On March 3, 1933, newly elected president Roosevelt closed the banks in response to the run on the gold reserves at the Federal Reserve Bank of

New York. By the time the banks reopened on March 13, there was no more gold to redeem. A few weeks later, Roosevelt ordered Americans to turn in their gold (except that used for jewelry), in exchange for paper currency, under penalty of imprisonment. The resulting influx became the gold reserves at Fort Knox, the depository for the world's largest stock of gold.

Incidentally, prior to his time as an economic advisor, Paul Volcker's role in the government had been to protect its gold supply. Volcker's department was tasked with confiscating any gold entering the country without a proper permit and upholding the Gold Reserve Act, which prohibited private ownership of gold. The act also allowed the United States to pay its debts in dollars, not gold, and established a new ratio of gold to dollars at a fixed price of thirty-five dollars per ounce.

Adding to the complexity of Volcker and Nixon's decision was the status of the dollar on the world's stage. In July 1944, near the end of World War II, delegates from the Allied countries had been invited to convene in the small mountain town of Bretton Woods, New Hampshire, to reach an agreement for a new international monetary system in hopes of fostering prosperity. The economy in the United States was in relatively good shape, compared to most of the war-ravaged countries in Europe, and the US government was flush with gold. Accordingly, the dollar was more stable than comparable currencies. Seven-hundred-thirty representatives from forty-four countries reached a consensus that the dollar would be the official reserve currency of the world.

Countries began pegging the value of their currency to the dollar instead of gold. The Bretton Woods Agreement gave foreign governments the ability to swap their dollars with the US for physical gold at any time at the fixed rate of thirty-five dollars per ounce. This clause provided assurance that dollars were literally as good as gold in the eyes of foreign governments. Most countries would never need to exchange their currency for gold; just knowing that the option was available gave enough peace of mind. As long as the dollar's convertibility to gold held, the dollar would remain the de facto world currency and would be universally recognized as an acceptable currency for any country to pay debt owed to another.

Consequently, the demand for US dollars increased throughout the world, affording Americans the ability to borrow more freely and purchase goods from overseas. In 1960, the United States held gold reserves worth $19 billion, enough to cover the $18 billion in foreign dollars held overseas, but increased global trade soon began to skew the relationship. The more Americans bought from other countries, the more they increased the dollars in foreign banks and foreign governments around the world, which eventually created the imbalance facing US policy makers in the summer of 1971.

Paul Volcker's analysis led him to the uneasy conclusion that the only wise move for the United States was to officially close the gold window (to cease convertibility). Volcker didn't take the idea lightly. Abandoning the Bretton Woods Agreement, which had governed the world's economic system for the previous three decades, could be seen as an act of economic warfare.

Furthermore, if the action resulted in a decreased demand for the dollar it could cause weakness in the dollar and lead to increased prices for American consumers. Even worse, the dollar might fall in value so much that it would trigger widespread hyperinflation. It was a frightening proposition. Still, there appeared to be no choice but to protect the remaining supply of gold by cancelling the dollar's convertibility into gold and rejecting the United Kingdom's request to convert.

George Shultz, another advisor in attendance at Camp David, supported Volcker's thesis. The value of the dollar, he reasoned, would stand on its own merits. Shultz would later become Ronald Reagan's secretary of state and believed that free markets should decide the value of a currency based on supply and demand in the global economy. Trying to pin a currency's value to gold was a fool's game in the modern economy, Shultz concluded.

The plan to cancel convertibility wasn't unanimous. Arthur Burns, chairman of the Federal Reserve, was a staunch believer in the role of gold in monetary policy. Burns was the first PhD to chair the Federal Reserve and a well-respected voice in the administration. He expressed concern that breaking the link between the dollar and gold could lead to disaster and usher in massive currency problems for years to come. Burns lobbied instead for a simple devaluation of the dollar, which would allow foreign banks to continue to convert their dollars to gold but do so at a much higher price than thirty-five dollars per ounce.

Nixon listened, contemplating the potential political, rather than economic, ramifications of such a decision. He feared that Burns's proposal would be construed by political opponents as weak, a possible death sentence for Nixon's future reelection bid. The president was only fifteen months away from a second election campaign. A devaluation of the dollar so close to election season could seal his political fate. The personal risk was too great. Furthermore, a devaluation would put the administration on the defensive while igniting fears of central governments around the world that the dollar was unstable. Economically, Burns's idea might have worked, but politically Nixon couldn't agree with it. In contrast, if Nixon closed the gold window, he could put a positive political spin on it. By offering a strong, confident, and victorious message to the American people, Nixon could portray the decision as a positive for the American economy.

On a Sunday night, August 15, 1971, the president interrupted the popular TV show *Bonanza* with an unexpected press conference. What followed was a political spin for the ages, a victory speech rather than a response to a crisis. "We must protect the dollar from the attacks of international money speculators," proclaimed Nixon, referring discreetly to the United Kingdom's request for the conversion to gold. "We are going to take that action, not timidly, not half-heartedly, and not in piecemeal fashion. We are going to move forward to the new prosperity without war as befits a great people, all together, and along a broad front. The time has come for a new economic policy for the United States."

President Nixon announced add-ons, such as tariffs and wage freezes, in an effort to buffer the country from the international response. "I have directed the secretary of the Treasury to take the action necessary to defend the dollar against the speculators. I have directed Secretary Connally to suspend temporarily the convertibility of the dollar into gold or other reserve assets," Nixon added, dropping the bombshell near the end of his speech.

The broadcast lasted only twenty minutes, but it shocked the world. After the announcement, now known as the Nixon shock, the global financial system changed overnight, and the world would never be the same.

Wall Street applauded the move. The next morning the New York Stock Exchange rallied 3 percent. Paul Volcker wasn't in the country to see it. He had been designated by Connally as the international point man on this issue. Volcker left for London just a few hours after Nixon concluded his public announcement. The following month would consist of a whirlwind of meetings and press conferences for Volcker. The exposure elevated his status among central bankers and the press, and his honest and direct approach won favor and trust within the international finance community, groundwork that would serve him well in his future ventures.

As the dust settled after the announcement, it became clear to world leaders that a new framework would be needed to govern the global financial system. Just four months after the Nixon shock, decision-makers from ten countries met at the Smithsonian Institution in Washington, DC, to forge a replacement for the Bretton Woods Agreement. The Smithsonian Agreement was announced in December 1971 to establish currency pegs for the ten countries in attendance, effectively devaluing the dollar against each currency. Nixon considered the deal monumental, boasting to the press that the Smithsonian Agreement was "the most significant monetary agreement in world history."

Nixon greatly misjudged its importance. Because of speculators and trade imbalances, countries were unable to keep currency values in line, so they abandoned the agreement and allowed their currencies to float freely. Within a year, the agreement was over. But Nixon's attention had shifted to his campaign for reelection.

The economic fallout was already underway. Abandoning all ties to gold ultimately meant that the US government was free to print money and run deficits as needed without concern for the quantity of dollars held overseas. In the twenty-five years following the Nixon shock, federal deficits averaged more than 3 percent per year, ten times larger than in the twenty-five years preceding Nixon's announcement. The average rate of inflation was roughly double over the same timeframe.

Welcome to the age of monetary excess.

2

THE OIL STANDARD

I'm the guy that caused the lines at the gas stations.

— *William Simon, US secretary of the Treasury*

William Simon's plane touched down on Saudi Arabian soil in July 1974. The smoldering heat only intensified the pressure of his singular mission: secure a consistent buyer of US Treasury bonds.

Three years had passed since the Nixon shock. Gold prices had soared to $190 per ounce, up from the fixed price of $35 per ounce on the day of Nixon's announcement in 1971. Since that time, the price of gold had been allowed to float freely and demand for the metal had soared as a hedge against the weak dollar. Little was keeping the value of the currency from cascading downward and threatening its status as the world's reserve currency. The implications were unsettling.

The United States needed something to boost demand for the dollar; ideally, Simon would find a long-term partner that would commit to investing in US government bonds for years to come. The Middle East was an obvious place to start because of the region's increasing power and trade surplus from oil exports. Iran and Saudi Arabia held center stage. By Simon's calculations, at the current production levels Saudi Arabia had enough oil reserves to continue production for the next 150 years. Iran's reserves were substantially smaller. He estimated that the country had a couple decades' worth, maybe less. If the Saudis would commit to purchasing US Treasury bonds with the money from their oil exports, it would allow the United States to continue to borrow money while hopefully stabilizing the falling dollar.

Despite the facade of friendship with the United States over the previous forty years, relations with Saudi Arabia had recently become strained. One year earlier, in 1973, Saudi Arabia joined forces with the Organization of the Petroleum Exporting Countries (OPEC) and made a surprise announcement to freeze all oil exports to five countries, including the United States. The oil embargo was initiated in retaliation for support for Israel in the 1973 Yom Kippur War. The war, which originated in a land dispute, had led to an Arab attack on Israel. The fighting had been brief but bloody, with casualties approaching eighteen thousand in only nineteen days. Nixon had responded by pledging his support for Israel and appropriating more than $2 billion for the country, including money to supply weapons, prompting anger from the surrounding Arab countries.

"America's complete support for Zionism and against the Arabs makes it extremely difficult for us to continue to supply the United States with oil, or even to remain friends with the United States," Saudi king Faisal said in a televised interview in 1973.

The decision to freeze oil exports had a dramatic impact back in the United States. Without access to the oil from the Middle East, oil prices in the United States quadrupled in a matter of months, crippling the economy. The dramatic increase in gas prices played a role in triggering a recession in the United States and increased inflation. Food prices rose nearly 20 percent in 1974, as did prices of many other everyday goods.

Perhaps no one was more familiar with the issues facing the country and the role Saudi Arabia could play in helping it emerge from its troubles than William Simon. Prior to his time as US secretary of the Treasury, he had served as the administrator of the newly created Federal Energy Office. Known to many as the energy czar, Simon was best known for instituting gasoline rationing at the pumps, a policy he had been forced to implement following the oil embargo from the Middle East.

"I'm the guy that caused the lines at the gas stations," he said.

Convincing the king to invest oil profits in US Treasury bonds wouldn't be an easy sell, but if anyone could do it, it was William Simon. Simon understood bonds, and he had a knack for selling them. As a former bond-trading superstar at the investment bank Salomon Brothers, Simon had run the firm's Treasury- and municipal-bond desk, making millions personally and for the firm. At the time, Salomon Brothers was known for its collection of aggressive bond traders, epitomizing the Wall Street bad-boy culture of the 1970s and 1980s. The small investment firm practically created the market for mortgage-backed securities. Simon's ascension within Salomon Brothers had been rapid, as he attained partner status within only ten months. Many pegged him as a potential successor to the CEO, but he was passed over when the time came.

The specifics of Simon's meeting remain unknown, but he flew home with the deal he wanted and the United States needed. The Saudis knew a good deal when they heard one. Situated in the middle of the most hostile region of the world, the Saudis would gladly invest in US Treasury bonds, earning a decent return in the process, in order to enjoy the support and commitment of the strongest military in the world.

Saudi Arabia agreed to purchase Treasury bonds with a large portion of its oil profits every year in return for military protection. The deal would equate to tens of billions of dollars of Treasury bond purchases each year. Simon had single-handedly increased the global demand for US debt and the dollar, allowing the United States to continue running deficits and borrowing as needed.

There was a catch to Simon's deal with the Saudis: under the agreement, the purchases had to be kept secret from the public. Generally, the government sells Treasury bonds through a public auction with multiple bidders. The details are disclosed in regular reports available to other government agencies and ultimately the general public, but Simon had a plan to circumvent that transparency. Rather than name the Saudis directly,

Simon's Treasury Department would simply incorporate the bond sales into a larger category referred to as oil-exporting countries in order to avoid disclosing the details of the purchase. For years, the Treasury Department used this backdoor approach to sell bonds to Saudi Arabia without going through the formal Treasury auction.

Challenged by Congress in 1979, the Treasury remained mum on the details, citing a law that permitted individual purchasers to remain nameless. The secrecy of the deal between Saudi Arabia and the Treasury Department would remain intact for nearly forty years until the Freedom of Information Act forced the release of the details in 2016, which is the only reason the story is public knowledge today. Simon's deal was monumental, but it was soon upstaged by the next deal the United States struck with Saudi Arabia.

Shortly after the completion of Simon's deal, Henry Kissinger, the secretary of state of the United States, reached an agreement with the Saudi king to price all Saudi Arabian oil transactions in US dollars and only in dollars regardless of the acquiring country. The details on the agreement and the concessions given are remarkably vague.

The complications from such a relationship, however, would prove to be fraught with unintended consequences as the United States was forced to repeatedly engage in Middle Eastern conflicts over the coming decades. Nevertheless, the petrodollar system was a viable economic relationship that afforded the US great comfort in knowing that the dollar would remain in demand. As the major player in the oil market, Saudi Arabia was subsequently able to convince the other OPEC members to follow suit. By 1975, all oil sales in the world were priced in dollars, ensuring the importance of the dollar on the international stage.

The deal was a win-win for both countries. In addition to deepening the partnership with the world's strongest military, the Saudis correctly reasoned that the dollar pricing would provide leverage in foreign-policy discussions and lead the United States to side with the country on Middle Eastern issues. With the Saudis already investing their oil profits in Treasury bonds, getting paid in dollars merely removed the risk associated with fluctuating exchange rates.

With the deal, the dollar regained much of the power lost in the Nixon shock and reestablished its position as the world's most prominent currency. The government could continue to spend and borrow as needed with complete confidence that the rest of the world would finance it. Unofficially, the United States had successfully replaced the gold standard with the oil standard.

3

THE INFLATION BATTLE

My condolences on your promotion.

— *Milton Friedman, economist*

The average American needed $17,000 in 1979 to buy the same goods that $10,000 bought at the start of the decade. Despite the deal with Saudi Arabia, the value of the dollar had weakened considerably since the country severed convertibility to gold. Loose monetary policies by Fed chairman Arthur Burns had only exacerbated the problem. For American consumers, the impact of the weaker dollar was a shock at the cash register, as the cost of everyday goods increased at a dramatic clip.

The backstory behind the surge of inflation can be traced to the 1960 presidential election, which remains one of the closest in history. The election pitted a relatively unknown, but vibrant, forty-three-year-old senator from Massachusetts named John F. Kennedy against forty-seven-year-old Richard Nixon. From the start, Nixon appeared to have the advantage. He had spent the previous eight years in the White House as vice president under Dwight D. Eisenhower. Not only did he have the name recognition, but he had the pedigree. Nixon had ranked near the top of his class throughout his schooling, developed champion debating skills, and attended Duke University School of Law on full scholarship. He was well versed in the political arena and ran essentially unopposed on the Republican ticket.

Early in 1960, an economist named Arthur Burns warned Nixon that an economic slowdown was probable later in the year that could derail his campaign. Burns was a professor at Columbia University and the president of the National Bureau of Economic Research. More importantly, Burns was considered an expert on business cycles in the economy. He was also an ardent Republican supporter, having formerly served as an advisor to President Eisenhower. As such, Burns suggested that action could be taken in advance of the dip to delay the downturn. Nixon relayed Burns's recommendation to increase the money supply and increase government spending before the election, but his request fell on deaf ears.

As Burns predicted, in April, about six months before the 1960 election, the economy began to weaken. The downturn was relatively brief, but it was enough to sway potential voters from the incumbent party. Swing votes went to Kennedy, who won the election in dramatic fashion, carrying the popular vote by less than two-tenths of a percent.

Burns's warning was prophetic. Nixon blamed the main cause of the recession on Fed chairman William Martin's decision to tighten the money supply in 1959, thereby fueling a long-held dislike for the Federal Reserve by Richard Nixon. Eight years later, he would get his redemption by defeating Hubert Humphrey in the 1968 presidential election. A year after winning the election, Nixon rewarded Arthur Burns for his loyalty and previous warning by appointing him to serve as the chairman of the Federal Reserve.

Burns holds the distinction as the first chairman of the Federal Reserve to hold a PhD, but his tenure wouldn't be remembered for his academic insight. Burns and Nixon had witnessed firsthand the impact an economic downturn could have on a presidential election, and neither had any intention of letting it happen again. Shortly after taking the reins, Arthur Burns began engaging in abnormally loose monetary policies of money printing and low interest rates. In hindsight, it appears that Burns purposefully tried to juice the economy leading up to the 1972 election at a time when the economy didn't need such policies.

Bruce Bartlett, an economist, former policy advisor to Ronald Reagan, and Treasury official under George H. W. Bush, wrote, "Burns took most of the blame [for inflation] because he had been a renowned economist before joining the Fed. This made it impossible to believe that he simply didn't know better. Therefore, one is left with the inescapable conclusion that Burns used the Fed to help Nixon with full knowledge of the disastrous consequences for the economy."

Burns's loose policies served their political purpose: President Nixon was reelected in 1972. Burns appeared to take similar steps again leading up to the 1976 election, presumably to try to help Republicans retain control of the White House, but his efforts were unsuccessful; the Democratic candidate Jimmy Carter won the election.

"Economists now recognize the Nixon era as Exhibit A in how the adoption of bad economic policies in pursuit of short-term political gain eventually turns out to be bad politics as well," continued Bartlett.

Coupled with rising oil prices, Burns's policies were beginning to haunt the American economy with dramatically higher inflation. Across the country, prices of everyday goods were rising faster than incomes. With little incentive to hold savings in the bank, the prudent strategy was to buy everything at once rather than waiting for prices to rise further. The idea caught on quickly.

"'Never buy what you can't afford' was the admonition of our parents," Christopher Rupkey, an economist for PaineWebber, said. "Today the statement has been changed to 'you can't afford not to buy it'. Get your money out of the bank and spend it. Inflation gives the most to those with the largest pile of debt."

A feedback loop quickly developed in which consumers bought more because prices were rising, but the more they bought the quicker prices rose. Inflation was becoming a self-fulfilling cycle. Consumer borrowing doubled from 1975 to 1980, increasing by nearly $160 billion as people scrambled to make purchases on credit. The inflationary cycle was in full force.

Burns's tenure as chairman of the Federal Reserve ended when President Carter appointed G. William Miller, a Democratic Party supporter, to the position. Despite the persistent inflation, Miller continued with the easy-money policies, perhaps trying to mimic Burns's approach to juicing the economy for his own party's benefit. In less than a year, the rate of inflation in the United States reached 9 percent. The dollar continued its slide, falling by a third against the German mark and more than 40 percent against the Japanese yen during Miller's time in office.

To make matters worse, for the second time in the decade OPEC imposed an oil embargo against the US, doubling the price of oil. The country teetered on the brink of a serious recession as inflation hit double digits. President Carter's approval rating fell to a low of 30 percent, prompting a decision to clean house and fire his entire senior staff, including Chairman Miller, opening the door for a new chairman of the Federal Reserve.

With the country reeling from inflation, President Carter needed a Fed chairman the country could trust to act independently to address the falling dollar and fight the persistent inflation—someone who had dealt with a crisis before. Carter knew that his choice could define his entire presidency.

The phone rang at Paul Volcker's home on the morning of July 25, 1979.

Paul Volcker, one of the key analysts behind the decision to close the gold-convertibility window, had remained a public servant after completing his time at the Treasury. Volcker had been offered several lucrative positions with Wall Street banks; one with a seven-figure income, but he had declined all the offers. Instead, he had accepted the position of president of the Federal Reserve Bank of New York, one of the twelve branches of the Fed. While the position was extremely prominent, his salary of $120,000 a year was far less than Wall Street had offered.

Oddly, the promotion from New York Fed president to chairman of the Federal Reserve came with a 50 percent pay cut. As chairman of the Fed, Volcker would be making less than $60,000 per year. With his family still living in New York, Volcker rented a small one-bedroom apartment in walking distance from his office in Washington, furnished it sparingly with cheap odds and ends, and flew home to New York on weekends to see his family.

Old friends reached out to Volcker with mixed responses. "My condolences on your promotion," Milton Friedman wrote. Friedman, a Nobel Prize–winning economist, had come to know Volcker well. He understood the responsibility Volcker would assume and the criticism he would attract. But more importantly, Friedman understood full well the mess Volcker was inheriting.

"In a very general way, I thought I had some sense of what the problems were," Volcker said in an interview with the *New York Times*. "I did not have the sense that this was an ideal time—and certainly not an easy time—to become chairman of the board."

That was an understatement.

The Federal Reserve has two main weapons available in the fight against inflation: increasing interest rates or limiting the money supply. Increasing interest rates is likely to discourage borrowing, while limiting the money supply, in theory, restricts spending. Chairman Volcker was open to either method and ultimately used both to some extent, but he favored the strategy that called for raising interest rates. Part of his logic was based on consumer perception. Tinkering with the money supply can be opaque. It's generally unclear to the average American how many dollars are in circulation at any given time. Increasing interest rates, however, was more concrete. It was an obvious move that consumers and businesses could see and feel in their everyday lives. By increasing rates, Volcker believed he could slow the inflation cycle if he could constrict consumer borrowing and slow consumption.

The only real way to know how the economy would respond to rising rates was trial and error. In his first official meeting as chairman, Paul Volcker sent a message. In October 1979, the Federal Reserve raised interest rates by a stunning 4 percentage points in a single day, a move never attempted before in the history of the Federal Reserve. The move wasn't without its critics.

An editorial in the *New York Times* captured the feeling on Wall Street: "Mr. Volcker is a gambler. He is betting high with a poor hand. The entire nation needs to hope he beats the odds."

In March 1980, an announcement was made that a small penalty would be charged for extending additional consumer credit. Volcker didn't particularly like the idea, which had initially come from President Carter, but with interest rates already hovering near historical highs and the president's approval rating at a low point, Volcker knew he didn't have the political capital to disagree. The controls provoked a sharp economic reaction, and were lifted just ten weeks after they were imposed.

Volcker recalled, "Consumers suddenly thought they'd better not use their credit cards, or consumer credit at all. But they had bills to pay, and so they drew down their cash balances."

With the economy in shambles, President Carter's 1980 reelection bid failed and Republican nominee Ronald Reagan won in a landslide. All the while, Volcker continued hiking rates. In December 1980, the prime interest rate hit 21.5 percent. As consumers lost faith in the dollar, they turned to gold, the price of which had become something of a proxy for inflation. The price of gold skyrocketed to $600 per ounce in 1980, up from $35 an ounce less than a decade earlier. Volcker was still in search of the tipping point that would kill inflation. His policies were beginning to try the patience of even his most vocal supporters.

The decision wasn't as obvious as it now seems in hindsight, but President Reagan decided to reappoint Paul Volcker to Federal Reserve chairman. The interest rate hikes were finally having an impact. As the months ticked away, inflationary pressures slowly began to recede. The dollar began to strengthen as money began to flow back to the United States from foreign countries. The price of gold fell to around $400 an ounce by the end of 1981.

"I grew up and was educated in the period when advanced thinkers said a little bit of inflation was a good thing. People thought they were a little richer each year, the profits were always a little higher than expected, it's nice to have the price of your house going up," Paul Volcker told the *New York Times* in 1982.

"In fact," Volcker continued, "I think there is some truth to that, but it's got a big catch: There's only some truth to it so long as people are 'surprised,' implicitly or explicitly, by the inflation. Once they begin getting the sense that it's a game, and they're just trying to keep ahead of it but can't, then you've got an entirely different set of circumstances."

Paul Volcker was fast becoming a household name and something of a hero to many. When *U.S. News & World Report* ranked the most influential people in America, Ronald Reagan finished first. Paul Volcker was second.

A fishing trip to remote Montana raised Volcker's own awareness of his impact on the country. Volcker and a friend sat at a log cabin restaurant in Bozeman, Montana, examining a chalkboard menu. Motorcycles and pick-up trucks filled the parking lot. Despite the press coverage, Volcker doubted he would be recognized by patrons and was startled when three burly men approached his table.

"Excuse me, sir," said one of the men, pulling a ten-dollar bill out of his pocket. He extended his arm toward Volcker. "But I was wondering whether you could sign this, considering that it's only worth something because of you."

To Volcker, the encounter signified that his victory over inflation extended well beyond numbers on paper in Washington: it was recognizable to the common man.

4

FISCAL PHILOSOPHIES

Government is not the solution to our problem;
government is the problem.

— *Ronald Reagan*

Paul Volcker's rate hikes may have defeated the inflation issue, but the interest rates hikes had dampened the economy as well and led to high unemployment. President Ronald Reagan and his advisors searched for a plan to jump-start the stagnant economy. Two opposite schools of economic theory dominated the day, one that called for increased government intervention and spending and another that called for the exact opposite.

The origins of the debate between the two strategies began following the publication of a popular Great Depression–era book titled *The Road to Plenty*, coauthored by William Foster and Waddill Catchings, friends and former classmates at Harvard. Foster became an English professor and ultimately the president of Reed College in Portland. Catchings worked his way up the corporate ladder to become a leading financier at a small investment firm named Goldman Sachs. He nearly bankrupted the entire firm following the collapse in stock prices in 1929 when he was personally responsible for nearly $290 million in short-term trading losses. After resigning from the firm and divorcing his wife, Catchings found new life at another investment firm in 1937, Lehman Brothers.

Together, Catchings and Foster authored several economic books, but *The Road to Plenty* was their crowning jewel. In it, they argued that good economic times could continue indefinitely so long as spending remained strong. Spending, they claimed, was not only the key to a strong economy, but was also the most important way out of a recession. The source of the spending—government or private sector—was less important than the effect on the economy. If business spending slowed, it was the government's responsibility to increase expenditures to offset the slowdown.

The book made a great impression on an entrepreneur and banker from Utah named Marriner Stoddard Eccles. Eccles owned numerous banks and served as a director for several other large companies. In 1932, during the throes of the Great Depression, Eccles was asked to give a speech at the Utah State Bankers Convention. In his speech, Eccles declared, "There is only one agency in my opinion that can turn the cycle upward and that is the government."

Shortly thereafter, Eccles and forty-seven other experts were summoned to appear before the Senate Finance Committee to advise Congress on what steps they felt could be taken to lift the country from the Great Depression. None of the experts were as memorable as Eccles, as he confidently spelled out a five-part strategy calling for the largest government spending plan in history up until that time. Congress listened intently but did nothing.

A year after Eccles's congressional testimony, newly elected president Franklin Roosevelt turned to Eccles for answers. With no end to the Depression in sight, Roosevelt appointed Eccles as chairman of the Federal Reserve and proceeded to enact the massive government spending package Eccles had advised. The plan is now referred to as the New Deal.

During the rollout of the New Deal, another, more mainstream economic book was released that echoed the ideas put forth in *The Road to Plenty* but applied them to the Great Depression specifically. John Maynard Keynes, a rather arrogant British economist, published *The General Theory of Employment, Interest and Money* in 1936. Keynes theorized that government spending was a key variable in economic growth and recovery. The theory wasn't new, but Keynes told the story best. According to him, an increase in government spending would lead to economic growth, which in turn would lead to increased tax revenue and eventually offset the increase in government spending.

Keynes argued that increased government spending could have, and should have, been used at the onset of the Depression to temporarily off-set the fall in private demand and spending. The thesis wasn't necessarily groundbreaking, but it was convincing, and shaped the way economists and, more importantly, politicians viewed the economy. Several years into the Great Depression, Keynes's book was seen as the answer to the question most politicians were asking: "What should we have done?"

One important consideration in Keynes's theory was that the increased government spending during recessionary times would be accompanied by falling tax collection, resulting in a government deficit, which would increase the national debt level. Keynes argued that the increased debt could eventually be repaid by higher government revenues through increased tax collection after the economy recovered.

The apparent success of the New Deal, coupled with Keynes's analysis, fueled the fire for politicians in Washington. Saving became a dirty word for economists. Spend, spend, spend! That was the way out of a bad economy. Politicians happily embraced the thought that they could use taxpayer money to rescue the economy.

With Keynes's theories as the rationale, central bankers and government officials felt free to meddle in the economy, feeling justified that they could spur economic growth with borrowed money and increased spending. Keynes's ideas were so widely embraced and championed by Eccles and others that followers of the new school of economic theory were known as Keynesians.

In January 1971, seven months before the Nixon shock, President Nixon sat down with Howard Smith for a public-television broadcast to outline his plan for reducing unemployment and stimulating the economy. During his interview, the president outlined his plans to run a budget deficit in 1971 and 1972.

"I am now a Keynesian in economics," Nixon said with a laugh. Months later, with the United States untethered to the gold standard, Nixon would be free to embrace Keynesianism in its full glory.

Ronald Reagan, however, considered himself to be a fiscal conservative and saw the recent bout of inflation as a byproduct of the Keynesian approach. As a staunch believer in free markets, Reagan believed private business, rather than government, was the key to solving economic problems. His victory in the 1980 presidential election ushered in a new economic framework referred to in the media as Reaganomics, in which Reagan publicly rejected the idea of government intervention.

"In this present crisis, government is not the solution to our problem; government is the problem," President Reagan said in his inaugural speech.

Ronald Reagan's economic approach identified much more with an Austrian economist named Friedrich Hayek, whose views largely contradicted Keynes's. Hayek made a name for himself by publicly challenging Keynes's theory in a series of writings. He had seen how inflation had ravaged his own home country following World War I and feared that Keynes's approach of using government stimulus would ultimately lead down the same path.

In Hayek's view, governments lacked the complete collection of pertinent information needed to make informed decisions about the economy. He believed that no individual or small group of individuals making policy could possess the knowledge to make better decisions than that of businesses and individuals in the free market. Rather, Hayek thought it better to avoid government intervention altogether and let the free market make the adjustments regardless of economic conditions. Later in his life, Hayek embraced more nuanced views that tax cuts, private enterprise, and reductions in regulation were keys to igniting economic growth, rather than increased dependency on the government.

His views on the economy found support with future world leaders such as Reagan and United Kingdom's prime minister, Margaret Thatcher, both of whom corresponded with Hayek in his later years and drew inspiration from his writings. He was ultimately recognized for his contribution to economics and awarded with the 1974 Nobel Memorial Prize in Economic Sciences.

Faced with a stagnant economy in 1981, Reagan imposed sweeping tax cuts for businesses and higher-income earners. By providing tax cuts to the wealthy, Reagan believed, the wealth would "trickle down" throughout the economy. Optimism grew, and the economy began to improve: unemployment rates fell, interest rates declined, and the stock market began to rally. Reagan, however, hadn't yet worked out the details on the spending prior to cutting the government's tax revenue.

Hayek shared his thoughts on the Reagan tax cut: "The idea that cutting taxes can produce higher revenues is 'in principle' right, but neither he nor the advocates know at what level of tax rates that occurs. On the scale on which it is being tried, I'm a little apprehensive. I'm all for reduction of government expenditures but to anticipate it by reducing the rate of taxation before you have reduced expenditure is a very risky thing to do."

The Hayekian model of economic reform would have coupled tax reform with a decrease in government spending in order to avoid large deficit spending. As a candidate, Reagan had embraced such an approach, promising to shrink the government by abolishing the Department of Energy and Department of Education, decreasing foreign aid, and reducing subsidies. The campaign promises would prove to be easier said than done. Rather than eliminate the Department of Education, the government doubled its budget to $22.7 billion during Reagan's time in office, as did the budgets for Social Security, Medicare, and foreign aid. In total, entitlement spending jumped from $197.1 billion in 1981 to $477 billion in 1987.

Combined with the tax cuts, government deficits in America soared, as did the national debt. The government debt burden increased from $900 billion to $2.7 trillion under Reagan's watch due to the simultaneous tax cuts and spending increases. The rate of the increase of government debt was alarming. It had taken thirty-one years for the national debt to triple prior to Reagan's time in office. Reaganomics accelerated the debt boom and tripled the national debt in only eight years. Despite the increased deficit and debt (or perhaps because of them), Reagan's time in office is largely remembered as one of economic expansion.

While tax cuts and government spending increases were both economic catalysts, the strongest factor impacting the recovery was simply declining interest rates. On the date of his inauguration, the Federal Reserve's overnight lending rate sat at 19 percent. On the day Reagan left office, the rate was around 9 percent. The ten-percentage-point reduction in interest rates helped consumers and businesses alike during Reagan's term. After inheriting a horrendous economy with massive unemployment and record-high interest rates, the next eight years were almost certain to show improvement regardless of tax reform or spending programs.

In June 1987, Paul Volcker stepped down from his post as chairman of the Federal Reserve, announcing that he wouldn't accept reappointment. "After eight years as chairman, a natural time has now come for me to return to private life as soon as reasonably convenient and consistent with an orderly transition. Consequently, I do not desire reappointment," Volcker wrote in a letter to the president.

Volcker's time as chairman of the Fed would be remembered by historians for his victory over inflation, but his tenure was fraught with unintended consequences, as we will discuss in later chapters.

5

DEREGULATION AND INNOVATION

"A series of events occurred that were outside the norm."

— Martin Gruber, professor of finance at NYU's Stern School

Alan Greenspan was appointed as Paul Volcker's replacement as chairman of the Federal Reserve. Greenspan was a well-respected economist with a PhD and a long-held belief in free markets. As such, deregulation became a central theme in 1990s. The tone was set early in his tenure by repealing legislation governing the financial industry, beginning with the Glass-Steagall Act of 1933, which prohibited retail banks from involving themselves in investment banking.

Prior to the repeal of Glass-Steagall, the American banking system was more heavily regulated than its competition in Japan. Accordingly, Japanese banks had shown tremendous growth, eventually making up eight of the ten largest banks in the world. By repealing the act, regulators hoped of opening the door to new opportunities for retail banks, leading to an increased ability to compete internationally and ultimately stronger profits.

"Repeal of Glass-Steagall would respond effectively to the marked changes that have taken place in the financial marketplace here and abroad," Greenspan said in response to international competition. The deregulation in the US, however, would lead to increased complexity and risk for retail banks, ultimately playing a role in the Great Recession of 2008–9, which we will discuss later.

The movement toward deregulation continued in 1991, when the Federal Communication Commission lifted the restriction on commercial uses for a relatively new technology called the internet. Up to that point, the internet had been primarily used by governmental agencies for research and education. Allowing commercial use would open the door for businesses to sell goods to the far corners of the world.

The inception of retail sales on the internet had humble beginnings. The first known online transaction to be completed via credit card was the purchase of a CD featuring the rock musician Sting by a Philadelphia shopper from an online business in New Hampshire for $12.48.

Reporting on the event, the *New York Times* said, "The team of young cyberspace entrepreneurs celebrated what was apparently the first retail transaction on the Internet using a readily available version of powerful data encryption software designed to guarantee privacy."

The potential for global commerce appeared to be unlimited and investors eagerly awaited their opportunity to profit from the internet revolution. One of their earliest opportunities began with the initial public offering of Netscape, the first well-known internet browser. It was unclear exactly how the company planned to generate profit. At the time of Netscape's public offering in 1995, the sixteen-month-old company had generated total revenue of only $17 million and had no profit. It didn't matter. Netscape had the first-mover advantage and controlled 90 percent of the market for internet browsing. The stock initially was priced at $28 per share but hit an intraday high of $74.75 before closing the day at $58.25, giving the company a valuation of more than $2 billion.

"It was easy to use," says Josh Quittner, coauthor of *Speeding the Net: The Inside Story of Netscape and How It Challenged Microsoft.* "It made pages viewable to people. It unlocked this mysterious world for normal folks, and the whole world changed."

Excited investors bid up the stock price to $174 a share for the profitless company. The 520 percent increase over the offering price marked the unofficial beginning of the internet bubble.

One of the earliest commercial ventures on the World Wide Web was an online bookstore based in Cleveland, Ohio, called Book Stacks Unlimited in 1992. At the time, transactions didn't actually take place online: the website offered bulletin boards that presented a menu of titles, but the transactions were still completed over the phone or in person. Book Stacks Unlimited later became Books.com and was eventually acquired by Barnes & Noble.

Books and CDs were easy products to sell online. Each was simple to catalog, identical to others, and easy to ship, which provided relatively low barriers to entry to savvy entrepreneurs. One of the first truly successful internet companies was an online bookstore birthed in a garage in Seattle and known as Amazon.com. The company's founder, Jeff Bezos, believed that by using warehouses and an efficient distribution plan, he could offer consumers far more selection than their local retailers and offer online reviews to help consumers make their selections.

As the number of websites on the internet increased, a need arose for a company to organize websites in a searchable way. Yahoo.com launched in 1995 and offered an early solution for web surfers to sort websites by content without having to remember specific web addresses.

Virtual auction house eBay also made its debut in 1995 and offered an avenue for anyone to sell almost anything without having to create an online store. eBay offered a level playing field for those wishing to empty their garage or clean out a closet for money. An early programmer for eBay named Pierre Omidyar tested the site's reach by offering a broken laser pointer for sale. A day later, his broken laser pointer sold for $14.83. Omidyar contacted the seller to confirm that he was aware that the laser pointer was broken. "I'm a collector of broken laser pointers," the man replied. Classic eBay.

In 1996, eBay transactions totaled $7.2 million. The next year, sales totaled $95 million when small stuffed animals known as Beanie Babies became a strange obsession for collectors and accounted for the majority of the company's sales.

Mark Cuban's online-radio company, Broadcast.com, made headlines when it came to market in mid-July 1998 and shot up a record 249 percent on its first day of trading. eBay went public in late September 1998 and jumped 163 percent in its first day of trading. Social-networking site theGlobe.com began trading publicly in November 1998 and jumped 606 percent on its first day of trading, surpassing Broadcast.com's short-lived record. InfoSpace, a twist on the traditional yellow pages, offered the final fireworks in December 1998 with its stock rising 45 percent on the day of its initial public offering. The company's stock would rise from $15 to $1,305 over the coming fifteen months.

The 396 such companies that had their initial public offering in 1998 raised more than $50 billion. Many of the businesses had no profits and never would. To many investors, it didn't matter. There was money to be made in the market, and investors' appetite for risk grew with each initial success story.

Amazon's Jeff Bezos was named *Time* magazine's person of the year in 1999 following the company's expansion into products beyond books and CDs. Amazon stock hit $110 in the spring of 1999, up from $1.95 on the day of its public offering. A $10,000 investment in Amazon at such time, would have netted nearly $565,000 over the following two years.

Retail investors weren't the only ones paying insane prices. Mergers and acquisitions picked up steam as tech companies started buying one another. America Online (AOL) bought Netscape for $4.2 billion in the spring of 1999. Yahoo bought GeoCities for $3.6 billion even though it was largely unclear what business model would allow the company to ever produce a profit. GeoCities.com, which allowed users to set up their own personal website, was the third-most-visited website on the internet. Yahoo also acquired Broadcast.com, which was also unable to show profits, for $5.7 billion.

The mother of all bad deals was announced in January 2000 when AOL and Time Warner announced a merger. At the time, the combined value of the companies came to roughly $300 billion despite having less than $1 billion in operating profit.

The tech boom and the US stock market peaked a month later.

Forty-four different dot-com companies ran ads in the 2000 Super Bowl, including Pets.com, the poster child for the insanity of the dot-com bubble. Pets.com went public in February 2000 at the peak of internet mania. Its total revenue at the time was less than $700,000. The entire company was liquidated 268 days later after losing $147 million in just nine months.

No single event triggered the bursting of the technology bubble, but prices began to fall rapidly in the spring of 2000. Over the following two months, the Nasdaq, a technology-centered stock index, fell 40 percent. The index had risen roughly 400 percent over the previous four years. After a brief recovery, the index fell another 50 percent through April 2001. Amazon stock fell from $110 a share to less than $7. Infospace fell from $1,305 to $2. Yahoo stock fell 95 percent to $4 in September 2001 from a peak of $125 only eighteen months earlier. eBay stock fell nearly 80 percent, but the company survived, which was more than could be said for many other dot-com companies.

In all, the Nasdaq index declined nearly 80 percent from its peak, bottoming in the summer of 2002 and erasing more than $5 trillion of shareholder value. According to the *New York Times*, 52 percent of dot-com companies that existed in 1999 didn't survive until 2004. The AOL/Time Warner merger was a complete disaster. More than $200 billion of shareholder value was destroyed as the company's share price plummeted.

Arguably, the most impactful meltdown of the dot-com era belongs to a company that had nothing to do with the internet. A small hedge fund in Greenwich, Connecticut, with less than one hundred employees, made more money than Disney, Nike, and Dell combined in 1996. The firm was bankrupt two years later.

John W. Meriwether made a name for himself as the head of the bond-arbitrage desk for Salomon Brothers in the 1980s. The division was relatively obscure within the investment firm, but it was highly profitable. Few outside the arbitrage desk truly understood what the traders actually did. Even fewer knew the inner workings like Meriwether.

Having overseen the division for years, Meriwether felt confident he could create his own firm and replicate similar investment results without having to share profits with Salomon Brothers. In 1993, Meriwether founded Long-Term Capital Management (LTCM) along with some of his most talented bond traders from Salomon Brothers. The firm recruited academics from MIT and Harvard to become partners. Long-Term Capital even attracted two future Nobel Prize–winning economists to join its staff: Myron Scholes and Robert Merton.

Together, the partners spent their first year at the firm traveling the globe in search of high-net-worth investors. Few investors understood Long Term Capital's actual investment strategy, a detail that didn't matter to most. The important consideration was that the LTCM partners were smart and confident. The commitments rolled in from business owners, celebrities, universities, other financial institutions, and even the Italian central bank. In total, the partners raised more than $1 billion in commitments before making their first investment.

LTCM was structured as a hedge fund, an unregulated investment vehicle tasked with investing money for ultrawealthy investors without oversight from a government regulatory body. Most importantly, by structuring the company as a hedge fund, it could also use as much leverage as needed to fund its investments.

LTCM used a handful of different strategies to generate its returns, but one unique trait was central to most: Long-Term Capital Management rarely owned traditional investments such as individual stocks and bonds. Rather, the firm chose to use investments known as swaps and futures contracts, essentially placing side bets on the price movements of traditional assets.

A gambler wishing to profit from the outcome of an NBA basketball game wouldn't need to own the actual team to earn a profit; rather they could simply place a bet on the outcome of the game. If team A wins, for example, the gambler collects money. If team A loses, the gambler loses the wager.

Alternatively, rather than betting on the final outcome of the game, thereby resulting in a 100 percent gain or 100 percent loss, a savvy gambler may enter into an agreement with the fan of an opposing team to swap money for every point scored. Under such a hypothetical bet, the gambler may choose to pay one dollar for every point scored by team A and collect one dollar for every point scored by team B. A quick look back at past NBA games might reveal that the average margin of victory is a mere four points. Therefore, the gambler could safely assume that the average risk with each bet would equate to four dollars at the end of a typical game.

Such a strategy may even allow the gambler to wait until the game was in process before entering into a bet. By doing so, the gambler could delay his wager until one team trailed by a large amount, say thirty points, before agreeing to swap dollars for points on the belief that the trailing team will eventually rally and close the gap in points. The technical term for this strategy is *reversion to the mean*.

This was Long-Term Capital Management's playbook: wait for an extreme divergence from the usual, then make a large bet that the gap would close. A typical swap for Long-Term Capital might involve entering into an agreement to swap the return on one asset (say, Italian bonds) for the return on a similar asset (like French bonds) over a certain period of time. In such an agreement, Long-Term Capital would profit so long as Italian bonds outperformed French bonds. It didn't matter whether both bonds went up or down in value, so long as the Italian bonds' total return exceeded that of French bonds. Using historical norms as its guide, Long-Term Capital could study probabilities based on computer models to indicate abnormalities relative to the past.

Long-Term Capital employed this logic to structure (with varying degrees of complexity) dozens of bets that appeared to be low risk. To increase returns, LTCM employed leverage of as much as 30:1. In other words, at any time, the firm might have thirty dollars invested per dollar of actual capital. By placing several different bets at once, LTCM felt comfortable that the risk was manageable. However, with leverage of such a magnitude, a mere 3.3 percent decline in asset prices would completely wipe out the equity in the entire firm.

Free of any requirement to disclose information about its strategy, holdings, or leverage, LTCM was able to borrow massive amounts of money from a variety of different Wall Street banks. Each bank happily extended billions of dollars in credit with little to no collateral, largely unaware that multiple other banks were extending the same credit.

LTCM enjoyed success right out of the gate, posting a 40 percent gain in 1994, its first official year of operation, prompting *Businessweek* to write an article introducing the "Dream Team" to the investment world. The firm followed up the stellar year by earning 55 percent in 1995 and a staggering 71 percent in 1996. Early investors, thrilled with their returns, happily doubled down, adding as much as they could. The partners bought in too. By the end of the year, each partner had invested a substantial amount of their personal net worth into the fund. 1997 proved to be slightly more challenging, but the fund still managed a return of 17 percent.

In the summer of 1998, LTCM's computer models identified Russian government bonds as a mispriced asset. The Russian economy was struggling from slumping oil exports, resulting in a dramatic decline in tax revenue. Government bond yields surpassed 30 percent as bond prices fell. For LTCM, it appeared to be a classic opportunity for prices to revert to the mean. The firm placed bets using swap contracts to profit from the pending recovery in bond prices.

Russia's government faced a difficult decision. It could continue to raise rates and borrow money to finance the deficit, or it could print more rubles and risk dramatic inflation. Russia opted to continue increasing interest rates. Borrowing costs surpassed 50 percent in May 1998. As bond prices fell further, LTCM increased its bet.

Behind the scenes, the central bank of Russia worked feverishly to maintain the value of the ruble against the dollar, buying rubles on the open market with the dollars it held in reserve. The central bank's currency reserves dwindled to $8 billion in August 1998, down from $20 billion the previous summer. Unwilling to continue using the shrinking pool of dollars, the Russian government stopped supporting the ruble, triggering a freefall in the currency. Strapped with unbearable debt and high interest rates, Russia made the surprising decision to default on a portion of its government bonds; an outcome for which the Long Term Capital's computer models hadn't accounted.

Russia's debt was payable in its own currency, the ruble. In theory, Russia could have simply printed more rubles rather than default. Long-Term Capital's computer models hadn't considered the human element of choice. Rather, the declining government bonds prices had appeared to signal an excellent opportunity to revert to the mean and LTCM had bet heavily on the outcome.

At the beginning of 1998, Long-Term Capital had $4.6 billion in actual investor capital backing more than $100 billion of investments. By September, the value of Long-Term Capital Management's holdings had declined by nearly $4 billion, erasing nearly all of the firm's equity. Investor losses were staggering. With such a small amount of remaining capital, the firm was leveraged at more than 100:1. More concerning for the overall economy, however, the investments, known as derivatives, were spread across the banking system. If LTCM failed, it wouldn't be able to make good on its end of the swap contracts.

Concern grew that an LTCM bankruptcy could dramatically destabilize markets and threaten the solvency of the US banking system. The Federal Reserve was ultimately made aware of Long-Term Capital's massive leverage and decided to intervene. The fear of such a chain reaction was likely unfounded, but it wasn't a chance that the Fed was willing to take. The New York branch of the Federal Reserve summoned sixteen prominent financial institutions to meet and discuss a plan for rescuing LTCM in hopes of avoiding a banking crisis.

The chosen bank executives crowded around the table at the Federal Reserve offices in New York discussing alternatives. When the dust settled, fourteen of the sixteen agreed to support a bailout effort, raising $3.6 billion collectively. The two banks that refused to participate in the bailout were Bear Sterns and Lehman Brothers. The decision didn't earn either many friends on Wall Street, and it would come back to haunt them later. With Wall Street's support, LTCM was allowed to survive long enough to unwind its bets and the firm was eventually dissolved without further incident.

"A series of events occurred that were outside the norm," Martin Gruber, professor of finance at NYU's Stern School said. "These catastrophes happen. The fault isn't with the models."

As it turned out, the real genius of the LTCM partners was getting the investment world to believe they were geniuses. The main lesson learned from the incident was that some institutions were simply "too big to fail." A new phrase was born on Wall Street.

When challenged about a lack of regulation, Fed chairman Greenspan offered his take: "I know of no piece of legislation that can be passed by Congress that can prevent [banks] from making dumb mistakes."

Long-Term Capital's meltdown went largely unnoticed by most retail investors, who still clamored to buy any stock with ".com" in the name.

6

CREATIVITY IN FINANCE

Just put it on your books and enjoy the money.

— *Tom Savage, AIGFP mathematician*

Technology stocks weren't the only stocks soaring in the late 1990s. The stock price of the insurance giant AIG rose 31 percent in 1998, 35 percent in 1999, and then another 42 percent in 2000. Unlike the profitless dot-com companies, AIG had actual earnings and a tremendous growth rate for a large, well-established insurance company. Net income rose from $3.7 billion in 1997 to nearly $5.7 billion in 2000, a large increase for a company selling insurance policies.

AIG had been busy with its own innovation during the tech bubble. In 1998, AIG essentially invented the world of the credit-default swap, which Warren Buffett would later refer to as a "weapon of mass destruction." These swaps would nearly sink the entire global financial system a decade later.

AIG's problems began in 1987 in a similar manner to LTCM's: a Wall Street hot shot left his firm to start a new firm using more exotic investments known as derivatives. By all accounts, Howard Sosin was brilliant. At age thirty-five, he was head of the junk bond desk at the investment bank Drexel Burnham Lambert, a firm known for essentially inventing the market for junk bonds, better known as high-yield bonds. Drexel Burnham Lambert had become Wall Street's poster boy of leverage and excess.

The firm's success in the bond markets had helped Sosin become a wealthy man, but he wanted more or he wanted out. Either way, in 1987 Sosin and a couple of select associates began planning their exit from Drexel to focus on the relatively untapped world of swaps—the same swaps that would eventually play a role in the demise of Long-Term Capital Management.

Swaps can be used in a variety of ways to either add risk or mitigate it. Initially, swaps were created as a way to hedge risk by providing some form of insurance. For example, if company A expects a large payment in euros, but reports earnings in dollars, it might consider hedging the risk of euro depreciation by entering into an agreement to swap euros for dollars at a preset rate. Company B may have the inverse situation and wish to swap dollars for euros. Neither company is speculating on the future value of either currency; they are merely hedging their respective currency risks by agreeing to swap the currencies at a preset rate in the future.

The ability to hedge away bizarre risks in currency, commodity, and stock prices wasn't new to Wall Street, but up until the late 1980s the terms of most swap contracts were set for a relatively short period of time. Sosin and his colleagues envisioned their new firm creating complex swap deals that could last for decades. It was a unique niche and potentially a lucrative one. It's not overly important to understand the details of this strategy; what's important is that Sosin was trying to disrupt a small corner of the investment industry by creating a way to provide longer-term insurance on investments.

To make that dream a reality, Sosin would need to form a partnership with a larger institution, preferably one with deep pockets and a great credit rating. Such a partnership would allow the new firm to structure deals at a lower cost than rivals, a key to Sosin's plan. One name topped the list: American Insurance Group, or AIG. AIG was massive, boasted an AAA rating, and was considered one of the world's strongest financial institutions.

After several meetings with Sosin, AIG agreed to form a new subsidiary known as AIG Financial Products, or AIGFP for short. Ten of Sosin's coworkers from Drexel Burnham Lambert followed him to AIGFP. Ironically enough, the firm's headquarters was located in a small office in Greenwich, Connecticut, just down the street from the offices that would later become home to Long-Term Capital Management.

Tom Savage was a mathematician who joined AIGFP in 1988. "Everyone kind of understood what the nature of the game was. This was not a company that involved speculating," Savage said. "So, it was everybody's job to criticize and double-check other people's opinions about what was appropriate business and what wasn't."

Shortly after opening its doors, AIGFP closed a $1 billion interest rate swap deal with the Italian government. The deal was monumental compared to the size of most swap contracts at the time. For its efforts and risk-taking, AIGFP earned $3 million, only 0.03 percent. AIGFP quickly earned a reputation as the most creative firm on the street, bringing in $60 million in revenue in the first six months.

While AIG enjoyed the revenue AIGFP was creating, few understood the complexities of each deal, and executives cringed at the freedom that had been granted to Sosin and his colleagues. Most concerning was that AIGFP was able to book its profits upfront and receive annual bonuses despite the long-term risk of deals that could span decades. If one of its deals went south, it would be AIG's problem to fix.

As the years passed, tension grew between Sosin and the upper management at AIG over the compensation structure. In 1993, Sosin left the firm, receiving a severance package of more than $180 million. With Sosin gone, AIG was able to reach a new agreement that called for AIGFP to defer a portion of its compensation to a later date, an agreement that more closely matched its own deal structures.

In time, the transactions grew more and more complex, and the deals grew larger. Early in 1998, the firm stumbled upon an idea to create a new kind of swap, known as a credit-default swap, that would come to define

AIGFP. For a fee, AIGFP would agree to insure an investor against a default in another company's debt. On the surface, these swaps were simply another form of insurance, allowing a bondholder to reduce the risk of a bond default. Investors, however, quickly caught on to the idea that they could use credit-default swaps as a speculative way to bet on company defaults regardless of whether they actually owned the bonds they were insuring. Some investors came to view the credit-default swaps as the equivalent of purchasing life insurance on a stranger and profiting from the stranger's death.

Still, AIGFP had no concerns about its own internal risk. "The models suggested that the risk was so remote that the fees were almost free money," Savage said. "Just put it on your books and enjoy the money."

In 2001, a new CEO, named Joe Cassano, took the reins at AIGFP. Cassano didn't have the typical Wall Street pedigree: he was the son of a police officer, and a political science major from Brooklyn College. His aggressive style was perceived as argumentative, and he frequently berated office underlings.

"He was very, very good," said Edward Matthews, AIG vice chairman. "But he was arrogant. He told us that in no uncertain terms . . . that all of his people up there were smarter than anybody we had at AIG."

The guys at AIGFP may have been smarter than most, but they were no longer alone in the industry. Investment banks all over Wall Street began replicating AIGFP's business model, creating new swaps and unique hedging strategies. All the while, a tangled web of interconnectedness was developing between banks and investors taking opposing sides of various deals and buying insurance against one another.

Regulators were less enthusiastic about the complex innovations. Officials in Washington were raising concerns about the secrecy and opaque structure of the swap contracts. How could the risks be understood or quantified? How should the swaps be valued and reported to shareholders? The Long-Term Capital Management meltdown had introduced the country to the risks of such exotic bets, but no regulation had followed. Accounting scandals involving derivatives also made headline news as Enron, an energy company based in Texas, imploded partially due to the use of the complex investments. Despite the dangers, Federal Reserve chairman Alan Greenspan and others made it clear that they had no intention of regulating the derivative market. Greenspan felt that the contracts were helping to make the financial system more efficient by providing modern ways for companies to reduce risk.

In truth, few policy makers understood what a derivative contract actually was, and even fewer knew how to regulate them. Congress offered no clarification either. The Commodity Futures Modernization Act of 2000 had removed state gaming laws' oversight of derivatives and simultaneously excluded most swaps from Securities and Exchange Commission oversight. Freed from regulation, swaps and other derivatives had quietly become the Wild West of investing.

"By ruling that credit-default swaps were not gaming and not a security, the way was cleared for the growth of the market," said Eric Dinallo, of New York State's insurance department. "None of this was a problem as long as the value of everything was going up and defaults were rare. But the problem with this sort of unregulated protection scheme is that when everyone needs to be paid at once, the market is not strong enough to provide the protection everyone suddenly needs."

AIGFP embraced the freedom granted by Congress and began insuring more exotic debt instruments, such as mortgage-backed securities and pools of loans known as collateralized debt obligations, eventually exposing AIGFP to hundreds of billions of dollars of risk.

On a positive note, short-term profits soared.

7

BAILING OUT WALL STREET

"We need $700 billion, and we need it in three days."

— *Hank Paulson, US secretary of the Treasury*

Dick Fuld was one of the chosen few within Wall Street's inner circle who had been seated at the table of the Federal Reserve office in the fall of 1998 to participate in the Long-Term Capital Management bailout. Ultimately, Fuld had declined to involve his firm, Lehman Brothers, in the bailout. The decision hadn't been well received by his fellow Wall Street CEOs willing to risk their own capital for the sake of helping the broader banking system. A decade later, Wall Street would get a chance to return the favor.

Prior to Dick Fuld's arrival at Lehman Brothers, the investment bank primarily focused on the mundane world of structuring bond deals, a fairly predictable and stable business with somewhat limited growth prospects. Under Fuld, Lehman Brothers expanded its services to include merger deals, asset management, and ultimately mortgage origination.

In March 2008, Fuld was named to the *Barron's* list of the thirty best CEOs in the world. The article even went so far as to dub Fuld "Mr. Wall Street" for turning "a bond shop into an elite investment bank."

"Smart risk management is never putting yourself in a position where you can't live to fight another day," Fuld told *Barron's* magazine. The article wouldn't age well.

Fuld made his mark on Lehman Brothers by guiding the investment bank into the mortgage industry with the purchase of Aurora Loan Services, a company that made mortgage loans to borrowers with bad credit, known as subprime loans. In 2000, Lehman purchased another such lender, BNC Mortgage. In 2004, Lehman and its subsidiaries made more than $40 billion in subprime loans. By 2006, the firm was surpassing that total on a monthly basis.

Individuals previously unable to get loans were suddenly able to borrow money with little to no down payment. In many cases, loans were made with "teaser" interest rates that reset after a period of time. Popular television shows chronicled the drama and success of first-time real estate investors attempting to "flip" a newly purchased home for a quick profit. The easy access to loans offered by Lehman and other investment banks was feeding speculative investment in the real estate market.

Rather than holding the loans it made, Lehman sold them to other investment banks, pension funds, and investors. By selling the loans, Lehman was able to turn a quick profit and simultaneously remove the risk of default from its own balance sheet, a great risk/reward tradeoff.

Lehman's newfound love for mortgages didn't concern most of the experts. Alan Greenspan praised the "financial innovation" of the investment banks. The purchasers of the mortgages weren't concerned either. Interest rates had fallen dramatically following the bursting of the dotcom bubble. Investors, starved for yield, gobbled up the higher-yielding mortgage investments just as quickly as Lehman and other Wall Street banks could package them.

The final factor that made Lehman's plan so lucrative was the helpfulness of the ratings agencies, which were tasked with issuing independent credit ratings on each bond. Thanks to hefty fees from the investment banks, the rating agencies developed a habit of assigning AAA ratings to the subprime bonds, the same credit quality given to the safest bonds on the planet. These ratings gave the impression that the risk of default on the mortgage pools was practically zero. Furthermore, the AAA rating allowed banks to hold the mortgage bonds as "tier one" capital, an important classification used to measure a bank's strength by regulators.

Eventually, the market became saturated with the low-quality loans, and Lehman opted to begin holding some of the loans it originated rather than selling them to other investors. Seeing another opportunity to grow profits, Lehman Brothers, Bear Stearns, and the other investment banks petitioned the Securities and Exchange Commission to ease regulations on the acceptable amount of leverage that investment banks could use. The allowable leverage ratio increased to 12-to-1. For every dollar in assets, the big investment banks were allowed to have twelve dollars in debt. The "Bear Stearns exemption," as it was known, applied to only five firms: Merrill Lynch, Morgan Stanley, Goldman Sachs, Lehman Brothers, and Bear Stearns.

Lehman could use the increased leverage to hold higher-yielding bonds and mortgages. But the math only worked if the investments owned by the firm paid a higher interest rate than the cost of the money it borrowed. The higher-yielding assets carried an added level of risk, which Lehman and other investment banks dismissed.

Officials could see the bubble in real estate but struggled to control it. The Federal hiked interest rates more than 425 basis points (or 4.25 percentage points) from 2004 to 2006 to slow the rate of borrowing. Short-term rates increased in response, but longer-term rates remained low, an occurrence Alan Greenspan referred to as a "conundrum."

"Long-term interest rates have trended lower in recent months even as the Federal Reserve has raised the level of the target federal funds rate by 150 basis points. This development contrasts with most experience, which suggests that, other things being equal, increasing short-term interest rates are normally accompanied by a rise in longer-term yields," Greenspan testified in 2005.

In hindsight, Greenspan's conundrum was likely explainable by a trade imbalance with China. In brief, for decades, the US has consistently imported more from the rest of the world than it has exported, resulting in a trade deficit. By maintaining such a deficit, a substantial amount of dollars flows into foreign governments' coffers each year. The foreign governments, flush with dollars, routinely convert their excess dollars into longer-term US government bonds, driving down interest rates in the process.

From 2004 to 2006, foreign central banks invested roughly $900 billion from their countries' trade surpluses in US government bonds. The huge demand for bonds helped to drive down yields and keep persistently low long-term interest rates in place, which further inflated the housing bubble in the US. Regardless of the cause of the bubble, real estate speculation continued to grow, as did the leverage in the financial system.

By early 2008, Lehman's assets totaled $680 billion, backed by only $22.5 billion of capital. Lehman's leverage was close to 30:1, a far cry from what the 12:1 leverage ratio allowed. Like Long-Term Capital Management a decade earlier, Lehman Brothers could be wiped out by a minor decline in asset values. To reduce its risk, Lehman had entered into a series of credit-default swaps with the strongest insurer on the street: AIG. Of course, the insurance would be useless if AIG was also insolvent, a thought so farfetched that no one bothered to model the possibility.

In late 2007, the US economy began to slow, in what appeared to be the beginning of a garden-variety recession caused by rising interest rates. Real estate prices weakened. Unsold homes sat empty. Unable to get their asking rate, many borrowers found themselves unable to pay their mortgages. The foreclosure rate began to increase. The secretary of the Treasury, Hank Paulson, a sixty-two-year-old former Goldman Sachs executive, tried to reassure markets.

"I do believe that the worst is likely to be behind us," Paulson said in May 2008.

Paulson was either overly optimistic or unaware of the true scale at which banks and investment firms were leveraged. As real estate prices fell, the market for mortgages dried up. With 30:1 leverage, it didn't take long for Lehman to feel the pinch. In June 2008, Lehman announced a quarterly loss of $2.8 billion from the decline in asset values. Investors punished Lehman's stock, sending it down by more than half since the start of the year.

As the next earnings report approached, the demand for the mortgage-backed bonds almost completely disappeared. It was becoming increasingly apparent that Lehman Brothers needed help to stay afloat. Lehman would soon have to report the fair value of the massive pool of mortgages it held, which had fallen so significantly that the company was effectively insolvent.

Much as it did with Long-Term Capital Management ten years earlier, the Federal Reserve began working to find a buyer for Lehman, or at least an investor that could pump money into the investment bank. The Treasury and the Federal Reserve were clear on one point: they had no intention of providing government money to rescue the failing firm. Two potential foreign investors surfaced: the Korea Development Bank and the Investment Corp. of Dubai, each of which explored the possibility before backing out. Lehman's stock price fell below eight dollars per share, down from sixty dollars at the start of the year.

Time was running out for Lehman, as the firm's third-quarter results were scheduled to show another dramatic loss. The firm needed help fast. Treasury Secretary Hank Paulson contacted Bank of America CEO Ken Lewis with a specific request: "Buy Lehman." Bank of America sent a team to begin due diligence immediately and determine whether the mission would be a rescue or a suicide.

After just one day of research, Bank of America concluded that because of the firm's massive leverage, additional government assistance of $65 billion would be needed before it could agree to purchase Lehman. Government officials balked at the request.

That same night, CEOs from twelve leading banks were summoned to the offices at the New York Federal Reserve for a special meeting to discuss a rescue of Lehman. It was déjà vu for many of the attendees. Ten years earlier, in the fall of 1998, the same basic group had been seated around a similar table discussing the rescue of Long-Term Capital Management. The terms were different this time. LTCM had been rescued with a measly $4 billion. By all accounts, Lehman Brothers would need fifteen times as much, and Treasury Secretary Paulson had made it clear that the government had no intention of providing money for the bailout. The survival of

Lehman Brothers rested squarely on the shoulders of its banking peers on Wall Street, the same group that Dick Fuld had shunned a decade earlier.

Unfortunately for Lehman, Fuld had burned too many bridges on Wall Street to muster the support he needed. His Wall Street cohorts gave Lehman Brothers the same cold shoulder that Lehman gave to Long-Term Capital Management in 1998. Within twenty-four hours of learning the news that no package would be offered, Lehman Brothers filed for bankruptcy. With over $600 billion in assets, Lehman Brothers was the largest company to file bankruptcy in American history—six times larger than the next closest. All twenty-six thousand employees were immediately jobless.

"We explored all available alternatives to avoid a collapse of Lehman, but the size of its losses were so great that they were unable to attract a buyer, and we were unable to lend on a scale that would save them," said Timothy Geithner, the president of the New York Federal Reserve Bank.

On the same day as the Lehman bankruptcy, the investment firm Merrill Lynch announced that it was selling itself to Bank of America for a fraction of its value just a few months earlier. Making up for lost time, the credit-rating agencies began downgrading virtually everyone on Wall Street, including AIG. The downgrade felt like a death sentence to the insurance giant. AIG would need to come up with billions in extra collateral to cover potential claims, an impossible task in light of Wall Street's collapse. Investors suddenly questioned which other troubled firms might fall. Shares of AIG stock fell 50 percent in a day.

AIG informed Geithner and the Fed that it too needed assistance to stay afloat. Thirty billion dollars should buy some time. Maybe $40 billion. Few on Wall Street could offer help under the circumstances. Still, private-equity firms and other banks examined AIG's situation closely. JP Morgan's research came to a different conclusion: AIG needed closer to $65 billion if it wanted to remain solvent. One by one, the potential suitors bowed out.

Representatives from AIG had met with Geithner earlier to warn him of the potential disaster, even presenting him with a list detailing AIG's counterparty exposure. The multipage list provided a breakdown of the financial system's risk exposure to AIG, totaling a staggering $2.5 trillion. Geithner, however, was sidetracked by other issues at the time, like bailing out lending giants Fannie Mae and Freddie Mac.

The time had come to pay attention.

There was virtually no way AIG could come up with the $65 billion it needed to stay afloat, but AIG had seventy-four million policyholders in 130 countries, more than $1 trillion in total assets, and untold multiples of that in derivative contracts. AIG appeared to be the domino that couldn't be allowed to fall. A 3:00 a.m. conference call was scheduled with officials at the Treasury, the Federal Reserve, and AIG. Ultimately, the Fed and Treasury relented from their pledge not to use government money. Later that day, AIG received an $85 billion bailout from the Federal Reserve in exchange for a majority stake in the company.

The decision to bail out AIG marked an abrupt change in policy from just forty-eight hours earlier, when the Fed had opted to let Lehman fail. Hank Paulson's vocal stance against the use of taxpayer money for Lehman led many on Wall Street to question the sudden change in regards to AIG. Others defended the move as the best option.

"It would have been a chain reaction," said Princeton University's Uwe Reinhardt, a professor of economics. "The spillover effects could have been incredible."

Over the course of the next three weeks, investment banks Goldman Sachs and Morgan Stanley required bailout funding as well. Washington Mutual, the country's largest savings and loan bank, collapsed. Wachovia Bank was taken over by Wells Fargo. Plans for a massive government asset-purchase plan known as TARP were released, celebrated, rejected, reworked, and ultimately approved by Congress. The Dow Jones Industrial Average plummeted more than 30 percent in just three weeks.

"My goodness. I've been in the business 35 years, and these are the most extraordinary events I've ever seen," said Peter Peterson, former head of Lehman Brothers in the 1970s and cofounder of Blackstone.

Within a month, a who's who of the financial world stepped forward for similar bailouts. The complex mixture of subprime debt, leverage, and derivatives had wreaked havoc on the financial system. Investors looked to the Federal Reserve and government officials to restore order. Hank Paulson (the Treasury secretary) and Ben Bernanke (the chairman of the Federal Reserve who had replaced Alan Greenspan in 2006) approached Congress for further assistance.

Senator Sherrod Brown recalled the conversation. "We need $700 billion," they told Brown, "and we need it in three days."

The details behind the request were hazy at best. Paulson was requesting the ability to spend $700 billion of government money as he saw fit, free from congressional oversight. Congress bristled at the idea but eventually compromised with a new plan known as the Emergency Economic Stabilization Act of 2008. Rather than engage in formal bailouts, the Treasury agreed to buy bad mortgages from the banks and work with borrowers; potentially restructuring terms of the loans to assist struggling homeowners.

Within days of passage, the terms changed. President George W. Bush granted Paulson and the Treasury Department the freedom to provide capital directly to the banks as needed. Hank Paulson had his blank check. Free to do as they pleased, the Federal Reserve and the Treasury ditched the mortgage-purchase idea and began directly pumping billions into shaky financial institutions.

"We've been lied to," said David Scott, a congressional representative from Georgia, who summed up the feelings of most Americans.

8

BLOWBACK AGAINST BAILOUTS

I understand why people are frustrated. I'm frustrated too.

— *Ben Bernanke, chairman of the Federal Reserve*

The late economist Milton Friedman had a knack for simplifying important ideas. In a now-famous paper written in 1969, Friedman emphasized the importance of increasing the money supply when trying to stimulate economic growth. Friedman gave the example of a helicopter dropping money over a town. The money, he explained, would be hastily collected and spent. The increase in the money supply would flow through the economy and increase wealth as it would allow people to engage in economic transactions that wouldn't otherwise be possible.

Prior to his appointment as chairman of the Federal Reserve, Ben Bernanke echoed Friedman's idea as a viable method of stimulating the economy at a speech to the National Economists Club in Washington, DC, in 2002. "The U.S. government has a technology, called a printing press (or, today, its electronic equivalent), that allows it to produce as many U.S. dollars as it wishes at essentially no cost. . . . Under a paper-money system, a determined government can always generate higher spending and hence positive inflation," Bernanke said.

Prior to his time at the Federal Reserve, Ben Bernanke had enjoyed a middle-class upbringing in a small town in South Carolina with a population of only seven thousand people. From early childhood, he was obsessed with learning. By age eleven, Bernanke was South Carolina's spelling-bee champion and competed in the national championships until the word *edelweiss* eliminated him from the competition. For all his smarts, Bernanke stayed grounded by spending summers working construction jobs and waiting tables.

Bernanke landed at Harvard after a friend earned a scholarship and convinced Ben to join him. He embraced economics, earning an undergraduate degree and eventually a doctorate at MIT. Shortly after, Bernanke taught at Stanford and Princeton, where he studied Milton Friedman's research on the Great Depression.

"I am a Great Depression buff, the way some people are Civil War buffs," Bernanke wrote in 2000.

There was perhaps no one in the country better prepared to handle the Great Recession of 2008 than Ben Bernanke. His appointment to chairman of the Federal Reserve in 2006 was well received, but it wasn't a foregone conclusion at the time. Publicly, the choice had come down to two candidates: Bernanke and Martin Feldstein.

The decision between the two appeared to be a coin flip, with Bernanke getting the nod from President Bush. In hindsight, it was a fortunate outcome for a less-than-obvious reason. Although highly qualified, Feldstein's resume included time as the former director of AIG and a board member for AIGFP. Had Feldstein been tasked with bailing out his former company, it may have tainted the perception of independence of the Federal Reserve for decades.

Throughout the winter of 2008, the US banking system continued to bleed money and the Federal Reserve continued to provide cash transfusions. Citigroup, having already accepted a $25 billion bailout, came back for more and received an extra $20 billion after posting another gigantic quarterly loss. Bank of America received a $45 billion package; Wells Fargo, $25 billion; JP Morgan, $25 billion; Morgan Stanley and Goldman Sachs, $10 billion each. In total, more than nine hundred financial institutions received government aid during the crisis. Bernanke was finally getting to run his printing press.

Bailouts were even extended to the automobile industry. With the unemployment rate soaring, government officials chose to provide assistance to the failing carmakers in hopes of retaining jobs. The additional layoffs weren't worth the risk to the overall health of the economy. The government provided Ford, Chrysler, and General Motors collectively with $80 billion in support, receiving various forms of equity in return. Bernanke correctly believed that these equity stakes would eventually allow the American taxpayer to recoup the vast majority of the bailout costs. The company-specific bailouts offered a tourniquet to the bleeding patient, but they didn't speed up the recovery time. Despite the potential costs to taxpayers, more capital appeared needed to unfreeze the economy.

In late November 2008, Bernanke announced an additional $600 billion asset-purchase program. The plan, which would come to be known as QE, short for quantitative easing, called for the Federal Reserve to purchase assets from retail banks. Critics took aim at the strategy for being eerily similar to the failed approach taken by the Bank of Japan in the 1990s, which will be discussed in more detail later. In this case, the assets purchased by the Federal Reserve would primarily be the bad mortgages weighing down bank balance sheets. In addition to relieving the banks of the toxic assets, the Federal Reserve hoped to provide additional liquidity to a market starved for buyers and thereby unfreeze the banking system. The Fed began by purchasing $100 billion of toxic mortgages from Fannie Mae and Freddie Mac, followed by another $500 billion of bad mortgages from the rest of the banking system. In December, the Federal Reserve moved interest rates into unprecedented territory by lowering the federal funds target rate to near zero in an attempt to stimulate borrowing.

"The Federal Reserve will employ all available tools to promote the resumption of sustainable economic growth," the official Fed statement read.

Government officials weren't taking any chances. In February, following President Obama's inauguration, Congress passed the American Recovery and Reinvestment Act of 2009, a $787 billion spending bill that provided money for health care, education, and infrastructure and offered various tax incentives.

"We are running out of the traditional ammunition that's used in a recession, which is to lower interest rates," said President Obama. "It is critical that the other branches of government step up, and that's why the economic recovery plan is so essential."

Not all government officials shared the enthusiasm.

"Yesterday the Senate cast one of the most expensive votes in history," Senator Mitch McConnell, the Republican minority leader, said following the passage of the 2009 stimulus plan. "Americans are wondering how we're going to pay for all this."

By the spring of 2009, the Fed had purchased, lent, or created more than $2 trillion. Never before had so much stimulus been thrust on the US economy, or any economy. Economists watched the great experiment with bated breath. The US government would be purposefully spending over a trillion dollars more than it received in tax revenue, generating the largest deficit in history. The budget deficit was exactly the economic medicine prescribed by economists following the Keynesian economic theory, which called for increased government spending to offset the decrease from the private sector.

For this Keynesian approach of deficit spending to work, the US government would need continued demand for government bonds. If demand for the dollar or government bonds wavered, the deficit spending could turn into a crisis. Fortunately for the United States, the rest of the world was enveloped in crisis as well, which led to increased demand for safe assets like government bonds. The strategic deals put in place decades earlier by William Simon and Henry Kissinger also provided a cushion. Saudi Arabian oil profits were still being invested in government bonds, and the rest of the world still priced oil in dollars. The combination of factors supported the continued demand for dollars and government bonds.

A somewhat-forgotten prerequisite for Keynes's theory to work in the long run is that the deficit spending must be temporary. At some point, a government must stop running deficits and slow the expansion of debt.

If not, the government would be left to continuously borrow, creating a massive debt burden that would be too large to repay.

For many American taxpayers, the long-term risk to America's fiscal health didn't justify the bailouts. The increased government spending was framed as temporary stimulus to get the economy back on track, but many saw the bailouts as just taxpayer money going straight into the pockets of Wall Street elites.

"I never was able to convince the average American that what we did with these rescues wasn't for Wall Street but it was for them," said Hank Paulson.

As months passed, the financial markets began to stabilize, but overall economic recovery remained slow, exacerbating a growing disconnect between the public and the government. Americans were increasingly losing faith in the government because of the intervention and poor oversight leading up to the crisis.

"I understand why people are frustrated. I'm frustrated too," offered Bernanke. "I'm not one of those people who look at this as some kind of video game. I come from Main Street, from a small town that's really depressed. This is all very real to me."

President Obama's approval ratings dipped from 67 percent at the start of his presidency in January 2009 to 49 percent by December 2009. Still, his approval rating was markedly better than that of Congress, whose approval rating fell to a stunning 25 percent by the end of 2009 according to Gallup polls, down from a 51 percent approval rating at the start of the decade.

Congressman Ron Paul became a vocal critic of the bailouts and the power held by the Federal Reserve. In 2009, he released *End the Fed*, a *New York Times* bestseller that portrayed the Fed as unconstitutional and oblivious to the best interest of the people.

"There is something fishy about the head of the world's most powerful government bureaucracy, one that is involved in a full-time counterfeiting operation to sustain monopolistic financial cartels," Paul wrote, "and the world's most powerful central planner, who sets the price of money worldwide, proclaiming the glories of capitalism," referring to Bernanke.

The media had a heyday assigning blame as well. A *Time* magazine feature, "25 People to Blame for the Financial Crisis," included Joe Cassano, Bill Clinton, Dick Fuld, George W. Bush, and even "American consumers." Alan Greenspan received criticism as well for his role in supporting deregulation of the banking industry and derivative markets. "Yes, I've found a flaw. I don't know how significant or permanent it is. But I've been very distressed by that fact." Greenspan conceded in a congressional testimony, "Those of us who have looked to the self-interest of lending institutions to protect shareholders' equity, myself included, are in a state of shocked disbelief."

Glenn Beck, an outspoken conservative talk show host for Fox News, frequently ranted about the perils of big government. In June 2010, he dedicated an entire episode of his show to a forgotten book titled *The Road to Serfdom*, which Friedrich Hayek had written during the throes of World War II.

Hayek's arguments against social planning resonated with the recent critics of the government bailout. The ideas, although arguably misunderstood, became a rallying cry for the right wing. Friedrich Hayek was making a comeback. His theories also came with a direct warning: if left unchecked, governmental policies would eventually impinge on individual freedoms, leading citizens to become overly dependent on the government; effectively becoming serfs, or slaves.

The public's interest in Hayek's work was resurrected overnight. *The Road to Serfdom* shot to number one on the Amazon charts within twenty-four hours of Glenn Beck's broadcast. By the end of 2010, the publishing company increased printing to seventy thousand copies a year, up from two thousand copies per year at the start of the financial crisis.

Reading Hayek is "kind of an 'Aha' moment for a lot of people today," said Beck. "Like Mike Tyson in his prime, [Hayek delivered] a right hook to socialism in Western Europe and in the United States."

As anger grew against the "establishment," extreme political sentiment began to boil to the surface in American politics. The Republican

Party gave birth to a movement known as the Tea Party, which championed the ideas of limited government, lower taxes, and reduced regulation. The name "Tea Party" was obviously a nod to the revolt that took place in Boston in 1773 in which colonists revolted against strong government and high taxation by dumping tea into the Boston Harbor. Ultraconservative members of the Republican Party harnessed the public's disappointment and touted a new line of thinking that resurrected some older ideas from the ashes. As discourse grew following the Great Recession, so too did anti-establishment ideals.

Ultimately, this new movement would lay the foundation for the 2016 presidential election, in which Donald Trump was victorious. Much of Trump's campaign rhetoric focused on limiting unnecessary spending, reducing taxes, and the general ineptitude of politicians and government officials.

9

THE SOLUTION

They're totally freaked out about Volcker.

— *Goldman Sachs lobbyist*

Slowly, the national discussion shifted from dealing with the crisis to preventing similar meltdowns in the future. The banking industry had been brought to the brink by investment speculation and risk-taking. It had been kept afloat by the government. It seemed clear that regulation would have to increase to avoid the same result.

Enter Paul Volcker—again.

Two decades removed from public office, Volcker was still among the most respected and trusted economists in the country. Since his time at the Federal Reserve, Volcker had bolstered his reputation even more by chairing a committee to investigate the Swiss bank accounts of Jewish Holocaust victims that remained dormant. His efforts resulted in settlements of $1.25 billion.

Despite being removed from the world of economics, Volcker had remained in tune with the financial situation and had strong feelings about what needed to be done.

"No one can reasonably contest the need for such reform, in the United States and in other countries as well. We have, after all, a system that broke down in the most serious crisis in 75 years," Volcker wrote in an op-ed to the *New York Times* in January 2010, describing his ideas for a solution. "To put it simply, in no sense would these capital market institutions be deemed 'too big to fail.' What they would be free to do is to innovate, to trade, to speculate, to manage private pools of capital—and as ordinary businesses in a capitalist economy, to fail," he wrote. The "too big to fail" mindset, Volcker argued, encouraged risk-taking and served as a potential detriment to taxpayers. Restrictions needed to be placed on banks in order to separate the riskiest speculation from the normal retail banking operations.

President Obama named the eighty-two-year-old as chairman of the president's Economic Recovery Advisory Board, an ad hoc committee designed to advise the president on the path to recovery. Volcker followed up his appointment with a three-page letter to the president outlining his proposal to deter the riskiest speculation. In January 2010, legislation aptly named the Volcker rule was proposed to limit proprietary trading and risk-taking in commercial banks.

Five former Treasury secretaries endorsed the Volcker rule in a joint letter published in the *Wall Street Journal*. "We fully understand that the restriction of proprietary activity by banks is only one element in comprehensive financial reform," the letter said. "It is, however, a key element in protecting our financial system and will assure that banks will give priority to their essential lending and depository responsibilities."

There was, however, one large problem with the Volcker rule. Prohibiting the riskiest activities of the banks would cost them billions in profits. In 2011, Reuters reported that Goldman's lost revenue from the Volcker rule could reach $3.7 billion. Goldman Sachs, Bank of America, and JP Morgan were vocal critics of the plan.

JP Morgan's CEO, Jamie Dimon, offered his thoughts on the Volcker rule. "If you want to be trading, you have to have a lawyer and a psychiatrist sitting next to you determining what was your intent every time you did something." He then offered a personal shot at Volcker, telling CNBC, "Paul Volcker by his own admission has said he doesn't understand capital markets. He has proven that to me."

"They're totally freaked out about Volcker," an anonymous Goldman Sachs lobbyist said. Goldman Sachs responded by hiring an all-star team of lobbyists, spending more than any other firm on Wall Street.

Goldman's political influence spread well beyond high-priced lobbyists. The firm had ties directly in the circle of the most powerful decision-makers. A quick rundown of former Goldman Sachs employees in the highest levels of government at the time includes Stephen J. Friedman, president of the Federal Reserve Bank of New York in 2008–9; William Dudley, who replaced Friedman as president of the Federal Reserve Bank of New York; Hank Paulson, the secretary of the Treasury in 2008; Neel Kashkari, assistant secretary of the Treasury for financial stability, who administered the $700 billion stimulus package known as TARP in 2008; and Gary Gensler, chairman of the Commodity Futures Trading Commission and formerly one of the youngest partners in Goldman's history.

Goldman had friends in high places.

"The individuals at Goldman have been incredibly powerful over time," said Hillary Sale, a law professor at Washington University in St. Louis who specializes in Wall Street regulation. "When you're a consumer, it gives you the creeps thinking about that kind of influence over regulation. But from the bank's side, it's a perfectly smart strategy."

With bank lobbyists involved, the bill known as the Volcker rule swelled to nearly three hundred pages of complex lingo and acronyms.

"I support the concept of the Volcker Rule," Peter Welch, a Democratic representative told the *New York Times*, "but these rules aren't going to be effective. We've taken something simple and made it complex. The fact that it's 300 pages shows the banks pushing back and having it both ways."

"I don't like it, but there it is," Volcker said when asked about the final version of the legislation that was now one hundredfold longer than his original letter to the president. "I'd write a much simpler bill. I'd love to see a four-page bill that bans proprietary trading and makes the board and chief executive responsible for compliance. And I'd have strong regulators. If the banks didn't comply with the spirit of the bill, they'd go after them."

The watered-down version of the Volcker rule passed in May 2010 and was scheduled to take effect in the summer of 2012, but extensions were granted as the deadline drew near. Exemptions were inserted. More extensions were granted. At the time of this writing, the rule has still not been fully implemented, nearly a decade after its proposal. Various changes to the rule have been proposed, the most recent of which, in 2018, called for simplified requirements for all banks and less restrictive requirements for smaller banks.

The Federal Reserve continued the accommodative policies set forth by Ben Bernanke in the years following the Great Recession. Quantitative easing (QE) was soon followed by further asset purchases in QE2 and QE3. The Fed's assets ballooned to more than $4.5 trillion by 2015, and the fed funds rate, the interest rate charged by banks to borrowing from one another, remained unchanged near zero.

Corporations took advantage of the low interest rates by borrowing money and buying back shares of their stock. Stock buybacks totaled more than $4 trillion from 2009–17 while corporate debt increased nearly $2.5 trillion. By purchasing stock on the open market, companies reduced the number of shares outstanding, thus spreading profits over a small base of investors, typically resulting in higher stock prices.

"We've been in a market bubble for a long time, and share buybacks are a big part of the bubble, made possible by artificially low interest rates that still exist today," said Peter Schiff, a financial commentator.

The stock market in the United States quadrupled from 2009 to 2018, but economic output remained sluggish, fueling further criticism of Fed policy.

"All it's really done is provide benefits to the wealthiest American individuals and corporations who don't really need the help," said Andrew Huszar, senior fellow at Rutgers Business School and former manager of the Fed's Agency Mortgage Backed Security Purchase Program.

The Federal Reserve wasn't the only entity trying to stimulate the economy. Government spending topped tax revenue each year from 2008 to 2018, resulting in record deficits and adding an additional $10 trillion in debt, bringing the current government debt load to $21 trillion as of this writing. More concerning is the rate of increase in government borrowing. Since 1971, government debt has ballooned from $400 billion to $21 trillion, a twenty-fold increase in nominal terms. Median household income in America, meanwhile, has only increased fivefold over the same period.

For years, the ballooning deficits and debts have seemed irrelevant. The US government has run a deficit in forty-four of the forty-seven years since formally severing ties with the gold standard in 1971. The United States has easily been able to support the increase in debt thanks to willing borrowers, a strong global demand for dollars (in part because oil remains priced in dollars), and reasonably low interest rates. For example, despite the increase in debt, the total amount of interest paid by the government in 2017 remained roughly the same as the amount paid in 2007. Even though the quantity of debt doubled, the effective interest rate was cut in half, making the burden easier to stomach and easier to ignore.

"There seems to be way too much pivoting away from the basic fact that we will have to make some hard choices to get our unsustainable national debt under control," said Maya MacGuineas, the president of the Committee for a Responsible Federal Budget.

Not everyone agrees.

In recent years, a movement has begun gaining attention known as Modern Monetary Theory (MMT). Loosely translated, MMT suggests that government deficits (and thus debt) are largely irrelevant because the US has issued debt exclusively in its own currency. As such, there is no possibility of a government debt default because the debt can be repaid by simply creating new currency. Therefore, deficit spending is of no concern and debt need not ever be reduced.

Furthermore, MMT suggests that governments have the ability to fund themselves without the need for tax revenue. Taxes should be viewed primarily as a policy tool to stimulate or contract certain areas of the economy.

In December 2017, the United States took another step to stimulate the economy by instituting a tax-reform plan to slash corporate tax rates in hopes of incentivizing spending and economic growth. Unfortunately, in 2018, the first year of the tax-reform plan, the budget deficit totaled nearly $800 billion, a 17% increase over the previous year.

Right or wrong, much of the current economy environment seems to filter through the lens of MMT. Debt and deficits haven't mattered for years. The dollar remains strong, interest rates and inflation remain low, while the stock market has continued to rally. Tax policies are viewed primarily as a method to stimulate the economy as opposed to a method of funding government spending.

Many well-known economists, including current Fed Chair Jerome Powell, have pushed back on the MMT theory. "The idea that deficits don't matter for countries that can borrow in their own currency is just wrong. I think US debt is fairly high as a level of GDP, and much more importantly than not, it's growing faster than GDP," said Powell.

Which economic theory is correct? Elements of each may be successful at different times in history. However, complex systems tend to be unpredictable, and economic history is fraught with well-intended policy mistakes. Regardless, when national debt expands faster than the economy, the likelihood of problems increases, the likes of which we may soon recognize in the US, Europe, China and Japan.

One truth stands out, as we will explore in the coming sections of this book: debt and deficits don't matter...until they do. And when they do... it's too late to avoid a crisis.

The Latin American debt crisis of the 1980s is a unique example that we will examine in greater detail in the next section.

PART 2

Latin America

10

THE BLESSING AND THE CURSE
OF OIL

They showed no foresight. They didn't do any credit analysis.
It was wild.

— *Angel Gurria, Mexican Office of Public Credit*

Latin America comprises three different regions: Central America (plus Mexico), the Caribbean, and South America, the last of which make up the bulk of Latin American countries. Unlike more developed economies, most countries in the region have a long history of dependence on commodity exports. When commodity prices are strong and global demand is high, the region's economies excel. The good times, however, have historically been followed by increased debt, which exaggerates the cycle, and amplifies the future problems when commodity prices eventually decline.

The king commodity for much of Latin America is oil, the importance of which can be traced back to the early 1900s and Winston Churchill's decision to swap the fuel source for the Royal Navy.

Churchill was named first lord of the Admiralty, the head of the Royal Navy of the United Kingdom, in 1911, shortly before his thirty-seventh birthday. The position would become a launching pad for Churchill's career, culminating in his ascension to prime minister of the United Kingdom a few decades later.

Churchill's reputation for making bold strategic decisions was born during his time as leader of the Royal Navy, and it proved pivotal in deciding the outcome of World War I, which began just three years after his appointment. Churchill oversaw the initial efforts of launching planes off of British ships, developing the armor for tanks, and improving the navy's tactical maneuvers against enemy submarines. His largest contribution, however, was the decision to switch the fuel source for the British navy.

Despite being well equipped with modern-day weaponry, British ships were relatively slow-moving, a huge disadvantage against Germany's increasing might. The German navy was undergoing rapid technological advancements, such as the newly effective use of the torpedo. Rumors abounded that the Imperial German Navy had even developed special submarines known as U-boats that covered large distances, boasted high-speed torpedoes, and burned kerosene.

Up until that point, the British navy was powered by coal, which was plentiful in Great Britain and nonflammable, a key feature in warfare. But oil burned hotter than coal, which afforded ships greater speed and maneuverability. Coal-powered ships were also easily visible from a great distance because of the black cloud of smoke produced by burning the coal, a problem not faced by oil-burning ships. Finally, coal-powered ships required substantially more manpower to refuel than oil-burning ships, which gave crew members less rest time while at port.

Churchill's predecessor, Admiral John Fisher, had been vocal about the possibilities of using oil to fuel the British navy since his time as first sea lord. "It is a gospel fact…that a fleet with oil fuel will have an overwhelming strategic advantage over a coal fleet," he wrote in 1902.

However, oil was far more combustible than coal and could erupt into flames during an attack. There was an even bigger problem. The United Kingdom didn't have oil. It had coal. Some officials even argued that there weren't sufficient quantities of oil in all the world to support such a dependence as that of the British navy. Churchill dismissed the concern but did ponder the logistics of acquiring the quantities of oil he needed.

"The oil supplies of the world were in the hands of vast oil trusts under foreign control. To commit the navy irrevocably to oil was indeed to take arms against a sea of troubles," Churchill wrote. Nevertheless, he moved forward with the conversion of the fleet.

Meanwhile, in Iran, a wealthy British man by the name of William D'Arcy was inadvertently solving Churchill's biggest problem. D'Arcy had made a fortune in the gold-mining industry and had become well known for his lavish parties and interest in horse racing. Around the turn of the century, D'Arcy, ever the speculator, agreed to fund an expedition for oil and minerals in the Middle East. He reached a monumental deal with the Iranian government, now known as the D'Arcy Concession, in 1901 that gave him and his company exclusive rights to explore for oil and minerals in Iran. The deal covered an expedition area of roughly 75 percent of the entire country. In return, D'Arcy agreed to pay 16 percent of profits to the Iranian government.

A few years into the search, D'Arcy's expedition was low on funds with virtually nothing to show for his exploration efforts. Resolute in his belief that he was on the right track, D'Arcy began borrowing money and taking on new investors to continue the search. Finally, with D'Arcy nearly broke, a drilling rig hit a gusher. On the morning of May 26, 1908, oil shot fifty feet in the air. D'Arcy had discovered enough oil to become fabulously wealthy yet again. The company he founded became known as the Anglo-Persian Oil Company and sold shares to the public in 1909.

Churchill persuaded the British government to become a controlling shareholder in the young company in 1914 and inject even more money into exploration. Years later, the British stake in the company would be renamed British Petroleum, or BP for short. With an adequate supply of oil at his disposal, Churchill moved forward with the conversion of the British naval fleet from coal to oil, which was completed shortly before the British were engaged in World War I. Thanks in part to the oil-powered ships, the swifter British fleet was able to hold its own against the German navy and survive the war.

The conversion of the British fleet was only the first step in the growth of the oil industry. The United States Navy soon followed suit, and Henry

Ford revolutionized the car industry with his assembly lines, furthering the necessity of oil for the advanced economies of the world. In a relatively short time, a simple commodity had become a powerful political and economic weapon. The sudden wealth from an oil discovery could change a country's fortunes for the better but could also lead to war or financial ruin if not properly handled.

Latin American serves as an excellent example. The region began producing oil commercially in the early 1900s and ramped up production throughout World War I. Mexico had been one of the top oil-exporting countries in the world at the time, but production fell dramatically following the Great Depression. Brazil, Argentina, and Venezuela, however, remained among the world leaders in global oil reserves.

Mexico's oil industry experienced a re-birth when a local fisherman named Rudesindo Cantarell Jiménez found and alerted the Mexican government about an oil slick he noticed on a fishing venture about sixty miles off Mexico's coast. Mexican officials investigated the source and discovered the second-largest oil reserve in the world, behind only that of Saudi Arabia. For his discovery, the fisherman was given a small lifetime pension from the government and the oil reserve was named in his honor: the Cantarell Reserve. Mexico's opportunity had arrived, one that the country hoped it could leverage into broad prosperity.

By the mid-1970s the world was divisible into two categories: countries with oil and countries without. As discussed previously, the importance of oil reserves grew with the Middle Eastern oil embargo imposed after the 1973 Yom Kippur War. Soaring oil prices transferred tremendous wealth from the countries forced to pay inflated prices for oil to the countries flush with oil reserves, especially those in Latin America, quietly benefiting from the drama playing out in the Middle East. In order to scale up quickly, Mexico was soon allocating nearly a fifth of all government revenue into oil and gas exploration.

US bankers took note of the promising conditions in Latin America and began competing to make loans in the region. Led by its CEO, Walter Wriston, Citibank became a leader in the push for international lending. Wriston was an aggressive leader with a knack for embracing financial innovation before the mainstream did. Citibank invested nearly $1 billion in the development of credit cards before showing any profit for the bank. Wriston also spurred the development of the ATM, a controversial idea at the time, but one that would catch on as a mainstay in the financial world. "The ATM has been the only useful innovation in banking for the past 20 years," Paul Volcker would later say.

In the late 1970s, Walter Wriston turned his focus to Latin America, and competition soon followed. Fearful of missing out, banks hired young salespeople straight out of college to travel to the far reaches of the world. Senior bankers, many of whom had never set foot in a Latin American country, found themselves scrambling to keep pace with the competition. Soon every major bank in the US had teams of jet setters in search of borrowers south of the border.

S. C. Gwynne is a *New York Times*–bestselling author. Before his career as an author, he was one of the jet-setting international bankers eagerly offering loans to Latin America. Gwynne's international banking career began in 1978, at age twenty-five, having had only eighteen months of banking experience on his resume.

"I am far from alone in my youth and inexperience," he wrote in an article in *Harper's*. "The world of international banking is now full of aggressive, bright, but hopelessly inexperienced lenders in their mid-twenties. . . . Their bosses are often bright, hopelessly inexperienced 29-year-old vice presidents with wardrobes from Brooks Brothers, MBAs from Wharton or Stanford, and so little credit training they would have trouble with a simple retail installment loan."

Even so, the bankers found themselves welcomed into Latin America with open arms. Borrowing from the American bankers offered an easy way to access capital, a privilege not routinely granted to underdeveloped countries and businesses. Brazil was a prime candidate for increased development, and the country began borrowing hundreds of millions of dollars. Initially, Brazil was able to claim fairly efficient use of the capital. The Brazilian government built highways, dams, and nuclear power stations. Factories sprang up that produced steel, chemicals, pulp, fertilizer, and even fuel from sugar-cane alcohol. The economy began to expand beyond its dependency on natural resources, and as the economy expanded, so did the borrowing.

The demand for oil reached a fever pitch in 1979, when tensions in the Middle East boiled over again. Spurred by both economic reasons and complex religious reasons, protests in Iran soon morphed into what's now referred to as the Iranian revolution. The drama spilled over into oil markets, resulting in production cuts. The price of crude oil more than doubled again, and long lines again formed at gas stations. For the second time in a decade, an oil crisis shook the global economy.

Mexico's oil discovery furthered its ability to borrow, and the economy strengthened throughout the 1970s. Economic development throughout the region also heightened competition in the banking industry. Loans came pouring into Latin America from foreign banks around the world.

Angel Gurría, head of Mexico's Office of Public Credit, marveled at the country's easy access to loans. "The banks were hot to get in," he recalled. "All the banks in the US and Europe and Japan stepped forward. They showed no foresight. They didn't do any credit analysis. It was wild." Gurría continued with an example. "In August 1979, for instance, Bank of America planned a loan of $1 billion USD. They figured they would put up $350 million themselves and sell off the rest (to other banks wishing to have loans in Latin America). As it turned out, they only had to put up $100 million themselves. They raised $2.5 billion on the loan in total."

The easy loans came as no surprise to Gwynne, the banker-turned-author. "When the senior VP asks how a certain country is doing in general, you don't say 'Well Phil, I think it's going down the tubes.' Even if it's true, it is not in your interest to say that, because Phil can easily make it impossible for you ever to develop a loan in that country. And your job performance is rated according to how many loans you make."

In many cases, however, the mounting loans weren't leading to increased development and improving infrastructure. Tangible projects accounted for less than half of the increased government borrowing throughout Latin America during the 1970s. In many smaller Latin American countries, spending on infrastructure actually decreased as a percentage of government expenditures despite the dramatic increase in borrowing. As time passed, countries in the region began to use the access to credit as an easy way to spend without concern. The increased oil prices were skewing government perceptions, and deficits and debt began to pile up.

The concern over excessive lending to Latin America wasn't lost on policy makers in the United States. Arthur Burns, the chairman of the Federal Reserve and former attendee at Camp David, offered his thoughts in a speech in 1977 at Columbia University in which he warned of the danger in excessive lending to Latin America. "Commercial and investment bankers need to monitor their foreign lending with great care, and bank examiners need to be alert to excessive concentrations of loans in individual countries," warned Burns.

His warnings fell on deaf ears.

11

RATE HIKES AND DEBT PROBLEMS

"Countries don't go bankrupt."

— *Walter Wriston, Citibank CEO*

In 1936, a Harvard professor named Robert Merton wrote a paper titled "The Unanticipated Consequences of Purposive Social Action." In the paper, Merton articulated a concept that came to be known as the law of unintended consequences. Loosely explained, the idea states that human action frequently leads to outcomes that aren't intended. In many cases, these unexpected consequences are negative, and other times there are surprising benefits. Occasionally the results are "perverse." The latter arises when the intended solution to a problem actually makes matters worse.

One example of unintended consequences occurred with the enactment of the Eighteenth Amendment, prohibiting the sale of alcohol in the United States. Originally, Prohibition was believed to be a way to clean up society and curb alcoholism. Politicians hoped to steer consumer spending toward less harmful consumer goods such as chewing gum, grape juice, and soft drinks. Patrons were also expected to substitute time in the saloon with time in the movie theatre or time with family. Real estate prices were expected to rise as neighborhoods were cleaned up.

Prohibition officially began on January 19, 1920. Over the next several years, the unintended drawbacks became obvious. Thousands of people previously employed in the alcohol industry found themselves out of work as breweries, distilleries, wineries, and bars were forced to close. The barrel-making industry evaporated, and transportation and shipping companies suffered. Many restaurants closed, unable to support themselves without alcohol sales. Entertainment and amusement industries declined. Tax revenue fell dramatically as well, even threatening the solvency of many states.

There were, however, some unintended benefits due to loopholes in the Prohibition laws. Legal exemptions of Prohibition were granted to pharmacists and churches. Pharmacists occasionally prescribed whiskey for ailments such as anxiety and the flu. In New York State, the number of pharmacies tripled during the Prohibition era. One such chain was founded by Charles R. Walgreen, whose name appeared on 20 small pharmacy stores in 1919. By the end of Prohibition, Walgreen's boasted 525 locations.

Churches were allowed to continue offering wine as a holy sacrament. Not coincidentally, church enrollment and attendance increased. Many states reported a surprising number of self-professed rabbis coming forward to obtain wine for their "congregations."

Prohibition laws also led to some perverse outcomes. Designed to clean up society, Prohibition actually moved the needle in the other direction. Organized crime dominated larger cities, creating platforms for mobsters like Al Capone. Corruption in the police force increased as well, with many in law enforcement accepting bribes for looking the other way or occasionally even joining in the bootlegging themselves. Underground markets sprang up and alcohol-related incarcerations increased dramatically. Most ironically, however, many historians point to an increased rate of alcoholism during the Prohibition era.

Paul Volcker's rate hikes that began 1979, aimed at reducing inflation, served as another classic case study in Merton's law of unintended consequences. The interest rate hikes ultimately put the brakes on inflation in the United States, but they also inadvertently sent ripple effects through the global economy. The impact was felt most dramatically by the Latin American economies, that had so freely borrowed money in light of the increased oil price.

Mexico's heavy investment in the oil industry had drawn it closer to energy independence, but it came at a dramatic cost. Public debt in Mexico increased tenfold from 1973 to 1981. More concerning, the majority of the loans were short term and only payable in dollars. In addition, the interest rates on most of the loans made weren't fixed, but floating, and changed with the prevailing rates in the United States.

As Volcker began his mission to end inflation in 1979, he was also inadvertently waging war on Latin American debt in the process. Interest payments increased dramatically with each rate hike, squeezing more money from Latin American governments and delivering it straight to the banks.

Thursday, August 12, 1982, was overcast in Washington. The early morning fog made the day unseasonably cool. A storm was brewing, but not one that would impact weather in the DC area.

Paul Volcker was in his office when the phone rang. He recognized the voice on the other end of the line as Jesús Silva Herzog, Mexico's Treasury secretary. The two had been meeting regularly over the previous months in private to discuss the precarious financial situation developing in Mexico. Their friendship had been cultivated over a mutual love for lemon meringue pie in the Federal Reserve's dining room, but their similarities extended well beyond a sweet tooth.

Herzog was Yale educated and well connected in the political circles that mattered. A briefing paper from the World Bank described him as a "politician of rare character. He has consistently fought for his convictions and does not hesitate to offer unpopular advice; tailoring opinion to please the powers that be is totally alien to him."

Like Volcker, Jesús Silva Herzog prided himself on honesty and transparency. At one point, Herzog even created a computerized system to try to prevent corruption within his department. It hadn't been well received by his fellow politicians. Despite that fact, he had been able to survive politically, partially because his father of the same name had been a well-respected Mexican economist. Family relationships aside, Herzog was effectively the Mexican version of Paul Volcker. Not surprisingly, the two had developed a good working relationship in recent months.

His tone on the phone was different now than it had been during their dinner conversations. Herzog had served as Mexico's Treasury secretary for only five months and hadn't fully realized the gravity of Mexico's bad financial situation before accepting the position. For all practical purposes, Mexico was broke. The country owed billions in payments within the coming months, all payable in US dollars, which Mexico didn't have.

Complicating matters further, the Mexican peso had weakened considerably since the start of the year, when Mexican officials opted to let the peso float freely without intervention. Twelve months earlier, twenty-five pesos could be swapped for one dollar. By August, it took nearly fifty pesos for every dollar. In terms of pesos, the debt burden had essentially doubled over the previous year. Herzog hung up the phone and boarded a plane from Mexico City to Washington that night.

He began the following day at the office of the International Monetary Fund (IMF). Originally established as a short-term lender and advisor to governments, the IMF effectively served as the international credit union of the world. The organization was capable of making small loans, but it hadn't dealt with a problem of this magnitude before. The Mexican government's total debt burden was more than $80 billion. The support Mexico needed would surpass any previous commitment in the organization's history. The majority of the IMF programs had supplied financing to developed economies such as France, Italy, Spain, and even the United States. The lending had been more out of convenience than crisis. Mexico's needs were different, but even more frightening was that Mexico wasn't alone. In fact, Mexico appeared to be the tip of the iceberg in Latin America.

The IMF informed Herzog that assistance could take weeks, perhaps months. Mexico didn't have that long. Herzog's next stop was at the negotiating table with the US Treasury Department. As a temporary stop gap, the United States offered to pre-purchase $1 billion of future oil from Mexico. To do so, however, Mexico would have to agree to stiff terms, including a $100 million fine and an effective 18 percent interest rate on the prepaid oil payments. Herzog called and pitched the details to Mexican president Lopez Portillo, who declined the offer based on the penalties and terms associated with the financing.

Herzog returned to the meeting and informed the Treasury that he couldn't accept the offer under the current conditions. Instead, he would have to return to Mexico without a deal, where he was prepared to default on the country's loans, which were primarily held by US banks.

Volcker, who had removed himself from the negotiations, stepped back in at the Treasury's request and took over. An agreement was reached to decrease the fine and lower the interest rate being charged to Mexico. Herzog flew home with the capital he needed to keep the country afloat for the immediate future.

Volcker spent his remaining time that weekend on the phone with other central bank officials overseas alerting them to the impending crisis. US banks weren't the only ones with loan exposure to Latin America. Japan had substantial capital at risk, as did select European countries. A default from Mexico could trigger a global banking crisis. Volcker's effort raised another $1.85 billion in temporary support for Mexico.

US banks were already aware of the growing debt crisis in Latin America, but the loans were too profitable to stop. In the previous year, foreign loans had accounted for more than 50 percent of all net profits for Citigroup, Bank of America, Chase Manhattan, Bankers Trust, and JP Morgan. Regardless of the risk, the loans had created insane profits for the banking industry. In fact, the increased perception of risk had simply allowed the banks to charge more. By the end of 1982, the top nine US banks had lent over 112 percent of their combined capital base to Mexico, Brazil, and Argentina alone. US bank loans to Latin America surpassed $100 billion.

In September 1982, Citibank's CEO, Walter Wriston, wrote an op-ed in the *New York Times* in an attempt to ease the markets. Countries "don't go bankrupt," he emphasized. In Wriston's view, countries shouldn't even be expected to reduce their debt; they simply need continued access to lending in order to refinance it. The problem, he explained, was one of liquidity. In other words, Latin American countries just needed more loans.

Wriston's op-ed calling for additional loans may have sounded crazy, but his point was valid. US banking regulations stated that banks were only required to show a loan as impaired after ninety days without payment. After such time, the impaired loans would have to be marked to "fair value" on the bank's balance sheet. The result would be billions of dollars in losses if Latin American countries couldn't continue to make their interest payments. However, as long as the borrowers were able to continue making payments, banks wouldn't have to show losses on their loans. Banking regulations said nothing about borrowers taking out additional loans to pay interest on previous loans. As ridiculous as the idea sounded, additional loans could be used as a temporary fix for a potentially disastrous problem. The Latin American countries, already strapped with unbearable debt burdens, would simply need to agree to take on even more debt.

Three months after the initial meeting with Herzog, the Mexican government reached an agreement with the IMF to establish a credit line of $4 billion that could be accessed as needed over three years. In exchange for the credit line, Mexico agreed to certain austerity measures aimed at reducing the country's cash flow shortfall. In short, the Mexican government agreed to slash public spending, raise taxes, and cut imports.

"This agreement enables us to avoid defaulting on our foreign debt of $78 billion," Herzog announced at the press conference.

Fear subsided that Mexico would default on its existing loans, which even incentivized some banks to offer additional loans to the cash-strapped country. In the few months since Mexico first requested help from the IMF, Argentina and Brazil had also come forward seeking similar assistance. The IMF had complied, extending a $2 billion line of credit to Argentina in exchange for similar cuts in government spending. Brazil was in a worse situation. From 1979 to 1982, Brazil nearly doubled its national debt. As rates rose in the United States, Brazil was already borrowing money just to make the interest payments on its mountain of debt.

Brazil's finance minister resigned in frustration. The country needed an additional $10.6 billion to service expiring debt.

With a population of 128 million people and a geographic footprint larger than the United States, Brazil seemed like the domino that couldn't be allowed to fall. The country's debt burden of $90 billion had become crippling, and previous (self-imposed) spending cuts had proved unsuccessful. The crisis was building steam, the debt was mounting, and the supply of funds from the IMF was limited.

Unlike central banks, the International Monetary Fund doesn't have the ability to create money. Instead, countries pay dues to be part of the IMF. These membership dues are used to fund loans to countries in need. In its simplest form, the IMF is tasked with lending money from rich countries to poor countries as needed. For practical purposes, the IMF doesn't simply hand a $1 billion check to a poor government. Rather, it provides the government with a credit line the government can use to access installments as needed. However, the loans typically come with restrictions on government spending, that must be agreed upon before accepting the credit line, which may be withdrawn at any point if a country isn't meeting the IMF conditions.

Throughout the following eighteen months, Colombia, Venezuela, Ecuador, Bolivia, Uruguay, the Dominican Republic, Chile, and Peru all stepped forward to request help. The conditional terms put in place by the IMF were unique to each situation, but generally focused on reducing government spending and increasing government revenue through taxation.

The spending cuts meant that each country accepting the conditional loans would be forced to sacrifice much-needed public services and forgo making investments in the country in order to repay the loans. The cuts were most painful to the poorest citizens relying on government assistance for health care, transportation, and education. In many cases, food subsidies were removed, sending costs of everyday items skyrocketing. Health clinics were unable to attain medicine, leaving no access to health care for millions. Schools closed because staff members weren't paid.

The mounting crisis was far too daunting for the IMF to solve alone. If banks stopped refinancing the debt as it matured, any one of the Latin

American countries could be forced into default, sending the whole region into panic and threatening the entire financial system. While this was understood within the banking industry, few Americans outside the industry paid any attention to the mounting drama.

Behind closed doors, many banks began to fear they were throwing good money after bad. With credit lines and austerity deals in place, the IMF continued to assure banks that the crisis would be managed. In reality, the IMF was buying time in the same way the banks had for years, by adding more debt to the mounting pile.

It was as if the whole region of Latin America had gone crazy borrowing money. Eager bankers had gladly paved the way with loan after loan despite the warnings. Now the debt-laden region saw no other option than to borrow even more money to keep paying the bills. Regardless, the tables had turned. The mounting debt was no longer a Mexico problem. It was a systemic banking problem. The writing was on the wall: this situation would not end well for someone.

12

LATIN AMERICA RESPONDS

*Unless you see it visually like this, you don't have
an appreciation of the problem.*

— *Edwin Meese, US attorney general*

Nearly half of all Peruvians lived in poverty in 1985, when the average income dipped to levels not seen in twenty years. The harsh cuts in government spending imposed by the IMF were taking their toll on the entire economy. The impact was felt especially hard in the health care sector. The ratio of doctors per person fell by more than one-third as health care professionals moved away from Peru or took higher-paying jobs in the private sector. The country's total headcount of nurses had also halved from the previous decade. Infant mortality spiked and the rate of infectious diseases tripled. Sadly, it became more common to die in infancy than of old age in Peru.

The crippled economy had also completely annihilated the value of the Peruvian currency, the sol. Earlier in the year, the decision had been made to convert the national currency from the sol to the newly introduced inti at a rate of one thousand sol per inti. Inflation soared as prices more than doubled for everyday goods.

The 1985 presidential election offered a glimpse of hope to Peruvians. A new presidential candidate with fresh ideas emerged as the front-runner. Alan García was only thirty-six years old, and Peruvians welcomed the fresh face and charisma with open arms. With little to lose, García campaigned on the idea that he would stand up to the IMF and fight back against its stringent requirements.

"We will try to go over the heads of the IMF and deal directly with the creditors, if this is possible," García told supporters in April 1985. "The fact is," García continued, "that Latin America cannot pay, and it cannot continue postponing its development. We have to explain this clearly and put our cards on the table."

García won in a landslide. Dubbed the Latin American Kennedy, Alan García was the youngest president in Peru in over a hundred years, and the youngest leader in the Western world at the time of his election. Up until his victory, Peru had followed the plan set forth by the IMF conditions and continued to make payments on its bank loans despite its crumbling economy.

No more.

García made a surprise announcement that Peru would begin making loan payments based on the strength of the country's exports. If the economy strengthened and Peru was able to export more goods and services, then the payments to the banks would increase; if not, then Peru would pay the banks back slower or not at all.

Almost three years into the crisis, García's plan was cheered as revolutionary. The Peruvian government was confident that the banks would be forced to accept the terms of the deal. García also believed he could convince the banks that it would be in their best interest to do so. Peru's strategy, however, meant that Peru would technically be defaulting on its loans, which would cause banks to report losses.

Four months after García's announcement, US regulators announced that banks would need to increase their loss reserves on existing loans to Peru and declared them "value impaired." Peru's credit rating dropped, and the flow of money into the country was essentially cut off.

Peru wasn't the first country in Latin America to miss a loan payment, but it was the first country bold enough to publicly speak out against the IMF and announce a formal strategy featuring a different payment schedule. Peru's debt load was too small to pose any real threat to the US banking system, but there was a growing fear that a larger country like Mexico or Brazil might follow suit.

Meanwhile, in Mexico the rate of inflation surpassed 100 percent. Every morning, plumbers, electricians, painters, and bricklayers gathered in the square across from Constitution Plaza in Mexico City in hopes of getting a day's work.

"Our goal is to survive, to be able to take home a little bit of money to our families at the end of the day," said a carpenter named Arturo Ochoa. "We don't want to be rich. We just want to be able to work."

"The number of people who are in the market for the kind of services we offer seems to be getting smaller and smaller," said Francisco Ruíz, a carpenter and father of eight children. "Either they do the work themselves, or else they simply can't afford to install a new kitchen or bathroom or even to repair the old one."

"Things were much, much better 20 or 30 years ago, because even though you were making less, it was possible to buy more with one's money," an electrician said in 1985. "When I retired, I received a pension, but it's only 40,000 pesos a month," he continued. "With the inflation we've had, you can't feed yourself for that amount of money, let alone a family, so I've had to come back to work." Plummeting exchange rates coupled with soaring inflation made the pension almost worthless, falling from roughly equivalent to $1,700 a month in 1980 to only about $100 a month in 1985.

In 1982, a Mexican worker could purchase one pound of chicken with the wages earned from about forty minutes of work based on minimum wage pay in the country. By 1986, the same pound of chicken required more than two hours' worth of wages. One pound of onions could be purchased after a mere seven minutes of work in 1982. By 1986, it took a full hour of work at minimum wage pay. Meat consumption fell dramatically throughout Mexico, and malnutrition began to rise.

"You eat less, and yes, there are some days you don't eat at all," said Mauricio Calderon, a plumber living with his in-laws.

"You buy whatever is cheapest," Ochoa said. "Nowadays we practically exist on a diet of beans, fruit, and a little noodle soup or a stew made of innards."

The country's woes deepened when two massive earthquakes registering 8.1 and 7.5 on the Richter scale hit Mexico City on consecutive days in the fall of 1985. The quakes killed ten thousand and left a hundred thousand more homeless. The capital was shell-shocked. The final tab for the quakes' destruction was more than $5 billion, leading Mexico to take on more debt in the wake of the disaster.

The earthquakes dealt a swift blow to the country's fledgling tourism industry. Several major hotels in Mexico City were destroyed, and those that remained struggled to attract visitors. Hotel occupancy in Mexico City fell to less than 10 percent of capacity. The value of the peso plunged to nearly five hundred pesos per dollar by the end of the year, down from twenty-five pesos per dollar at the start of the crisis. Meanwhile, Mexico's debt had ballooned an additional $16 billion and stood at an insurmountable $96 billion.

Shortly after the earthquakes, James Baker, the Treasury secretary of the United States, announced that he had a plan to solve the crisis, the first official solution set forth by the United States. The world listened as Baker pitched an idea that called for an additional $29 billion in loans to the region over three years. Although the countries were already strapped by debt, Baker reasoned that providing them more money would reignite their economies and allow them to grow out of their recessions. His plan was met with applause from the banking community.

"The president of the World Bank (A. W. Clausen) and the managing director of the International Monetary Fund (Jacques de Larosière) wish to express their strong support for the initiative which, given the urgency of the problems, should be translated into positive and concrete actions as soon as possible," a joint statement read regarding Baker's plan.

It almost goes without saying, but the additional debt failed to provide the relief intended. Observers placed blame for the failure on the banks for not lending more and on the Latin American governments for not getting their own financial houses in order. But the plan was flawed from the beginning, and the end result was simply more debt.

Despite its problems, Mexico was actually faring better than many of its Latin American counterparts. Inflation in Brazil topped 500 percent while Bolivian inflation soared to 50,000 percent in the spring of 1985. The Bolivian government finally quit making loan payments and stopped printing money entirely.

With virtually no available jobs, illegal (to the United States) emigration rose dramatically as Mexicans traveled north of the border. The emigration of affluent, skilled businesspeople, intellectuals, and artisans became so prevalent that the Mexican people coined a phrase to describe the phenomena: "la fuga de cerebros," translated as "the flight of brains."

"I can't prove it, but it seems to me Mexico is losing some of its most aggressive young people," said Alan Eliason, chief of the United States Border Patrol station in San Diego. "It's not the weakest ones that are making the trek up here: they're exporting some of their best and their brightest. We are definitely getting more educated people in the flow, occasionally even government employees," he added.

Rafael Rodriguez, a twenty-four-year-old marine biologist, offered his take: "A street sweeper or a dishwasher in the United States earns more than a brilliant professional here. You can't buy a house. You can't buy a car. Your wife has to go to work just to make ends meet. A lot of people just end up saying, 'I can't go on living in this system,' and opt for living overseas."

For those who stayed in Mexico, however, there was one booming industry: the drug trade. With limited money to pay police, the illegal drug trade became the easiest source of income for many. The drug industry in Mexico directly employed an estimated fifty thousand people in the mid-1980s. With more than 10 percent of the US population partaking in recreational marijuana and cocaine, the Drug Enforcement Administration estimated total US drug consumption to be $110 billion, roughly equal to Mexico's entire national debt. Although the numbers aren't widely known, it is believed that the drug trade brought in nearly as much revenue to the Mexican economy as the country's oil exports.

With the economy in shambles, the narcotics industry attracted many of the highest-skilled laborers, including the country's limited number of biologists, botanists, and geneticists. The main players in the drug industry were perceived by many in Mexico as modern-day Robin Hoods. By mid-1986, Mexico was the largest supplier of marijuana and heroin to the United States.

Peru quickly cornered the market on cocaine. By 1987, Peru had become the leading producer of cocaine in the world, supplying nearly 75 percent of the global output. The Huallaga Valley, about two hundred miles north of Lima, became ground zero for Peru's production. With over one hundred thousand acres planted with coca, the area is more than twice the size of Napa Valley's acreage dedicated to growing grapes.

US attorney general Edwin Meese visited the Huallaga Valley for a firsthand look. "Unless you see it visually like this, you don't have an appreciation of the problem," Meese said, following his helicopter flight over the valley.

Meese marveled at the valley as he crossed mile after mile of farmland planted with coca. Harvested leaves sat in the open waiting to be dried, ground, and processed into cocaine. Children waved enthusiastically to the passing helicopter, and farmers made no effort to hide. Law enforcement was virtually nonexistent. "The most vivid scene to me was looking at shack after shack with the coca leaves drying out in front," Meese said. "You can see today how manual eradication is not going to be effective."

Even though the drug industry was one of the only positive areas of Peru's economy, President García openly embraced efforts to eradicate the drug trade as a necessary step forward for the country. Soldiers were deployed into the jungles to find and destroy the labs, and civilian pilots sprayed fields with herbicides to kill the crops. However, with such extreme poverty throughout the country, helicopter pilots could be easily bribed. Many pilots reportedly accepted additional payment to swap water or fertilizer for the herbicide, completely negating the eradication effort.

American officials explored the idea of large-scale eradication efforts by using chemicals, but plans ultimately fell through when the manufacturer refused to allow its chemicals to be used for the purpose. Eli Lilly was afraid of the unknown ecological consequences from massive amounts of herbicide flowing into the wetland regions and rivers. The potential negative impact on livestock and Peruvian citizens wasn't worth the risk for the company.

The US and Peruvian governments also attempted to encourage voluntary crop substitution by co-funding a $25 million loan program for farmers in the area. The joint venture provided loans to coca farmers willing to switch to crops such as rice, sugar, or coffee. Unfortunately, the legal crops required substantially more work than coca production and yielded 60–80 percent less in monetary returns. Farmers participating in the loan program were unable to make enough money to repay the loans. It soon became obvious that the program meant to help the farmers ultimately did even more economic damage as farmers defaulted on the borrowed money.

13

ESCAPING THE LOST DECADE

Is he the smartest guy in the room? No.

— *Chuck Schumer, US senator from New York*

"These problems will be with us until the 1990's. We don't see anything in the global economy that will allow these countries to get out of these problems soon," John Reed, Citi's new CEO, warned investors in the summer of 1987.

A few months earlier, Brazil made a bold decision. Rather than continue with spending cuts, Brazil announced that it would abandon the IMF restrictions and simply stop making payments on its $113 billion debt load in hopes that creditors would renegotiate the debt and reduce their restrictions on the economy.

Eyes had turned to Citicorp, which was still a massive holder of Brazilian debt. For the first time since the crisis began, Citi was forced to restate the value of a small portion of its Brazilian loans. The bank cautioned investors that it could have losses totaling $3 billion, a mere fraction of its total loan portfolio.

Stockholders yawned. Citi's stock fell slightly on the news but rallied higher in the weeks that followed. Despite the problems in Latin America,

US banks had seen increases in their stock prices throughout the crisis. Citi's stock price had nearly tripled from the start of the debt crisis in 1982 to the summer of 1987.

As the months passed, it became apparent that banks were not willing to renegotiate as Brazil had hoped; the creditors would simply wait it out. Unfortunately for Brazil, the decision to halt payments had only created more economic uncertainty within the country. Foreign investment in Brazil fell dramatically while inflation remained over 100 percent. Internally, support from Brazilian citizens faded. The government finally relented and resumed payments in 1988. The bold plan had lasted less than a year. The Reagan administration and the IMF praised Brazil's reversal and warmly welcomed the world's eighth-largest economy back into their good graces.

Brazil had hoped that other Latin American countries would follow its lead and stop making loan payments as well, but none had. Brazil had been left to go it alone. A concerted effort by the Latin American countries to cease payments would have likely forced creditors to renegotiate terms. But no such effort was attempted. A series of meetings between the indebted countries had taken place in Colombia in 1984, but no cartel was ever created. Argentina had challenged creditors and the IMF for a brief time, but because it appeared their economies were improving, Brazil and Mexico didn't join the effort.

In 1985, Peru's attempt to tie debt payments to export earnings fell flat when other countries didn't do the same. In 1986, with its economy in shambles, Mexico nearly suspended all debt repayments, but Brazil and Argentina felt their situations were improving and didn't join forces. The banks had done a marvelous job of renegotiating small deals with each country throughout the process, careful to stagger the repayment incentives in an effort to avoid a concerted plan among the countries. Latin American countries eventually resigned themselves to the fact that there was no way out of the crisis.

Meanwhile, Peru was descending into chaos. In September 1988, the Peruvian government announced a 400 percent price hike on gasoline and a 100–200 percent increase on most food items. Beer sales fell by 90 percent. The economy had ground to a total halt.

Ester Moreno was the mayor of Independencia District of Lima. "Last year the government invested 100 million soles [about $2,000] in education in Independencia," she said. "What can you do with 100 million soles. . . . With some 28,000 young men of school age we can only offer vocational training to 80. Is it surprising we have a lot of juvenile delinquency?"

"Everyone is warning that we're heading for the abyss," a high-ranking Peruvian official said. "Yet nothing happens."

The rest of Latin America had little sympathy for Peru. It was doing no better.

Julio Garrett, Bolivia's vice president, said, "Bolivia is the country in South America where the IMF has imposed the most harsh and rigid conditions. No other country has been subjected to austerity measures that are so severe and inflexible; no other country has had to pay such a high degree of sacrifice and suffering in order to conform to the IMF."

Two out of every three Bolivians suffered from some form of malnutrition. One of every four children born in Bolivia died before their first birthday, and of those who lived, 10 percent suffered from brain damage because of insufficient nutrition. Despite the problems, the Bolivian government continued to reduce its health budget to meet IMF spending requirements.

The austerity efforts by the IMF had simply added more debt and forced governments to deprive their citizens of basic services. Someone needed a legitimate plan.

Enter Nicholas Brady.

Nicholas Brady was appointed secretary of the Treasury of the United States in the fall of 1988. Brady had enjoyed a long career working for an investment bank on Wall Street after graduating from Harvard Business School in 1954. By the 1960s, he was managing the firm's corporate-bond trading department. Eventually, Brady worked his way up to chairman and moved the firm into investment management, venture capital, and mergers and acquisitions.

Unlike most Wall Street executives, Brady wasn't "type A," extro-verted, or loud. He seemed to delegate everything, kept his opinions to himself, and rarely worried about the details. Brady also held a general dislike of excessive debt, and he wasn't a fan of the financial innovations of the 1980s. He campaigned against the high-yield bond market and the popularity of leveraged buyouts, which used massive amounts of debt to recapitalize companies before selling them to other investors.

"When the best and the brightest of this country are spending all their time on financial engineering, you're rearranging the deck chairs, rejig-gering corporations, just changing their shape, instead of laying long-term plans. When I went into business it was professional, where people had pride and standards," he said.

Brady was also more casual than most politicians. He was known to wear shabby sweaters, sit with his legs flung over the side of the chair, and avoid idol chit-chat without a purpose. Brady's distinctive approach was often mistaken for indifference, and his skills as an orator left much to be desired. The *New York Times* described Brady as "bland on television and awkward as a public speaker."

David W. Mullins, a Harvard professor, noted that Brady "has a unique ability to somehow encourage people to underestimate him." Brady made it through Yale as an undergrad but did so with a reading disorder that forced him to "read and reread things six times" to gain an understand-ing. Before beginning business school at Harvard, Brady visited a special-ist and learned that his reading level was on par with a seventh grader, but he was able to compensate for his weakness in reading by becoming a world-class listener. He learned to soak in information in oral briefings and lectures better than his classmates by listened intently and simplifying each discussion down to an understandable summary.

"He's the best sounding board an executive can have... I have yet to meet anyone who can match his talent for drawing a square around a problem," said Louis "Bo" Polk, chief financial officer of General Mills.

Those that knew Brady best described him as fiercely competitive, a trait that helped him become a stellar athlete during his days at Yale. "If there is a winning side and losing side to a game, he absolutely has to be on the winning side," said his wife, Kitty. "I mean, he can play tennis with little old ladies and be polite but he'd rather play to win."

Despite his accomplishments, Brady was relatively unknown outside of financial circles before October 19, 1987, when the US stock market plunged 22 percent in a single day. When the world of finance struggled for answers, President Reagan appointed Brady to head an investigation. The Brady Report surprised Wall Street with its depth and thoroughness, earning him praise outside his usual sphere of influence. Jeffrey Lane, the president of prominent investment bank Shearson Lehman Hutton, offered his praise: "In hindsight, the Brady Report was the most definitive of all the studies after October. In this business, he is known as one of those people who knows what is going on."

The report provided support for his eventual nomination and appointment as successor to James Baker as Treasury secretary. Now it was Nicholas Brady's turn to take a crack at solving the Latin American debt crisis, and he took a different tack from his predecessor.

"Treasury Secretary Nicholas Brady uttered the magic words last week: 'debt reduction.' He conceded that third world countries, heavily in debt to Western banks, needed relief," the *New York Times* reported.

Brady outlined the basics of the plan to a group of bankers, academics, and former government officials at a conference known as the Bretton Woods Committee, named after the famous 1944 agreement. The plan was met with mixed reviews.

"Is he the smartest guy in the room? No. I'm not sure I agree with his plan, but at least he tried to do something," Senator Chuck Schumer said.

"We can't tell if the glass is half full or half empty," Senator Paul Sarbanes, a Democrat from Maryland, offered. "But there is water in the glass."

"It's clearly a step in the right direction," echoed Senator Bill Bradley. "But I didn't hear any magnitudes."

Former Treasury secretary James Baker wasn't quite so optimistic. "I believe this path leads both debtors and creditors off the cliff," Baker said. "This approach would irreparably politicize the debt problem." Baker had reason to be pessimistic: his own plan, enacted in 1985, had failed miserably, resulting in billions of dollars of extra debt with no tangible improvement.

The new plan, which quickly came to be known as the Brady plan, encouraged banks to swap nonperforming loans for new longer-term, lower-yielding debt. The new debt would be secured by government bonds, thus ensuring payment and liquidity. By agreeing to the swap, banks would effectively be forgiving a portion of the balance owed.

The indebted countries would benefit from a reduction in debt, a more favorable interest rate, and a longer repayment schedule, providing much-needed cash flow relief. One issue still needed resolution: the plan needed financial backing to refinance the mountain of debt one last time. An unlikely benefactor emerged and agreed to ante up to make the plan work in the summer of 1989: Japan.

"Actually, we're happy to call it the Brady plan," said a Japanese financial official when asked about the name. "But perhaps with an asterisk that it's backed by Japanese money."

Over the prior decade, Japanese banks had become substantial holders of Latin American debt, even surpassing the exposure of American banks by 1989. "It used to be said here that the debt problem in Latin America was a United States problem," another Japanese government official said. "The Japanese used to view the Latin American debt crisis as a fire on the other bank of the river. Recently, that has changed."

Over the next five years, roughly 30 percent of Latin American debt across eighteen countries was effectively forgiven under the Brady Plan. Finally, able to reduce their annual payments, many countries found relief from the crippling debt that had burdened their economies throughout the 1980s. Spending on basic necessities such as health care and education resumed, and the economies began to grow again as life improved throughout the region. The "lost decade" was finally coming to an end in Latin America.

14

NAFTA AND THE PESO

You Americans sell, we Mexicans buy.

Shopper at newly opened Walmart in Mexico

Globalization was a key theme in the 1992 US presidential election. One of the main points of contention was a pending trade deal between the United States, Canada, and Mexico. The incumbent, President George Bush, had already begun negotiations to create a free trade zone that would remove trade barriers and tariffs in North America, but he was unable to finalize the deal before the election. The North American Free Trade Agreement, or NAFTA, became a focal point for candidates.

As the election neared, Ross Perot, an independent presidential candidate, became a vocal critic of the trade deal, describing the agreement as a zero-sum game. He represented the voice of Americans worried that without barriers to trade, millions of low-paying American jobs would be outsourced to Mexico. Perot repeatedly warned of a "giant sucking sound" of jobs leaving the United States for Mexico if the deal passed. His imagery resonated with voters, and support for NAFTA waned.

Bill Clinton, the Democratic Party's candidate and a former governor of Arkansas, viewed the deal through a different lens. Clinton was well acquainted with the potential benefits of globalization. The Walton family, founders of Walmart, had long been friends and supporters of the Clinton family throughout their ascension through the political ranks in Arkansas. In 1986, Bill Clinton's wife, Hillary, had become the first female board member in the company's history, a position she held until 1992, when her husband made his run for the presidency.

Clinton had the advantage of witnessing firsthand, the success of Arkansas-based retail giant Walmart had enjoyed from its early ventures abroad. In 1991, Walmart entered into a 50-50 partnership with Cifra, Mexico's largest retailer. Cifra already understood Mexican culture and had the operational expertise to handle the logistics throughout the country. Walmart had the name recognition and the size and scale to drive down prices for consumers. Their first venture together was a Sam's Club in Mexico City.

Bethany Moreton wrote about Walmart's entrance into Mexico in her book *To Serve God and Wal-Mart: The Making of Christian Free Enterprise*: "The opening day of the world's largest Wal-Mart was appropriate to the historical moment. Mariachi musicians and scantily clad spokesmodels were just the beginning. Someone in a penguin costume did the cha-cha across the slippery tile floor of the 244,000-square-foot Wal-Mart Supercenter while amused customers watched."

The Sam's Club in Mexico City had offered a glimpse of what was possible from overseas consumers, and Walmart was quick to support NAFTA and encourage policy initiatives that furthered globalization. Likewise, Bill Clinton remained supportive of the NAFTA legislation throughout the campaign and ultimately won the 1992 presidential election.

"When I entered the Clinton administration, there was a lot of excitement about what was going on in emerging markets," said Jeffrey Garten, undersecretary of commerce for international trade in the Clinton administration. "They were opening up to foreign investment . . . adopting capitalism for the first time. We were very excited about it and we pushed even harder for more opening."

Garten continued, "We got very geared up to help U.S. firms win market share. . . . We were quite convinced that what was going on was in everyone's interest, because the emerging markets that we saw wanted more investment, and their leaders were saying to us, 'We want to liberalize. We want to open these economies. That's best for our own growth,' and we thought we were pushing in exactly the same direction."

Not everyone shared the administration's enthusiasm. One key naysayer was Republican Congressman Tim Hutchinson, who echoed Perot's concern about job losses in the US. Hutchinson was particularly noteworthy because he represented Arkansas's third district, including Walmart's hometown of Bentonville, Arkansas.

Unable to find support from its own representative, Walmart urged its suppliers to write their representatives and encouraged them to get involved in the fight to approve NAFTA. The company leaders organized meetings with Secretary of the Treasury Lloyd Bentsen and US trade representatives. Walmart's corporate counsel even testified to the House Ways and Means Committee, pointing to its own success with Mexican consumers.

Walmart also took it upon itself to sway Hutchinson by offering a field trip to Ixtapalapa, Mexico, to visit the largest Walmart in the world at the time. Hutchinson accepted, and was able to see firsthand, the thousands of shoppers strolling through the aisles. Over half of the products on the shelves were American made: Fruit of the Loom socks and t-shirts, baby toys and soap, power saws and drill bits. Once Hutchinson saw the demand for high-quality American goods, he quickly became a convert and returned to the States with a new outlook.

"One of the real lasting impressions was the appetite for American products that exists in Mexico," Hutchinson said. His change of heart was a dramatic win for Walmart and other NAFTA supporters. Members of Congress were shifting into the pro-NAFTA camp as well.

Vice President Al Gore echoed Hutchinson's support: "They [Walmart in Mexico] have seventy-two cash registers ringing constantly with people in that country—in Mexico—taking American products out of that store."

Reports told stories of Mexican women on their "pilgrimage" to "this country's newest shrine: Wal-Mart," where customers happily gazed at "such exotic made-in-the-U.S. wonders as Rollerblades, microwave popcorn and upholstered cat perches."

"You Americans sell, we Mexicans buy," a female shopper was quoted as saying. "It is good for both of us, no?"

The tide of public opinion had suddenly shifted. The Mexicans were consuming vast amounts of American goods, and if the United States wouldn't provide the goods, surely Asia or Europe would.

"Failure to ratify the North American Free Trade Agreement could— I say could, not necessarily would—trigger a global economic collapse," warned a doomsday columnist for the *Boston Globe*.

With Walmart as the crowning symbol of free trade, NAFTA passed on November 17, 1993. Mexicans universally applauded the signing of the agreement in hopes that it would accelerate growth in the Mexican economy. Having suffered through the lengthy debt crisis in the 1980s, Mexico was finally beginning to show signs of life, and officials hoped the NAFTA agreement would signal to the rest of the world that the country was back on stable footing.

The general consensus among politicians and economists was that Mexico would be the country to benefit most in the long term from NAFTA because of the new job opportunities and increased foreign investment. Mexico, more than Canada and the United States, could offer cheap labor and seemed like a natural place to attract lower-skilled jobs. The construction boom of factories and plants was a foregone conclusion. The investment into Mexico would likely send interest rates down and set off an economic boom. Mexican borrowers were so convinced of the outcome that adjustable-rate mortgages became the loan of choice in hopes that their interest rates would adjust lower.

Then something unexpected happened. The two-sided free trade agreement become incredibly one-sided. American consumers didn't have an appetite for Mexican goods, while Mexican consumers happily scooped up all the goods and services that American companies could provide. K-Mart entered Mexico, as did Sears and Dominos. The American goods were made better. They lasted longer, they didn't break, and they cost about the same. There was no comparison. Mexican consumers began to choose the American goods over locally made products. Mexican

companies, struggling from the increased competition, began to close factories. Demand for the peso fell.

Following the debt crisis of the 1980s, Mexican officials made the
decision to adopt a fixed exchange rate. Rather than allow the dollar price
of the peso to change, the Mexican government intervened as needed
in the currency markets to keep the peso and dollar at a predetermined
exchange rate, a decision that offered certain benefits in trade and tourism.
An American tourist traveling to Mexico with $100 to spend would know
in advance exactly how many pesos to expect at conversion. Companies
engaging in international trade wouldn't have to navigate changing currency values with each transaction.

There is, however, one great downside to a pegged currency regime.
For a currency's value to remain constant, there has to be relative stability in the supply and demand for the two currencies, which are constantly
bought and sold in the open market. In Mexico's case, as the demand for
American goods rose, so too did the demand for dollars. To keep the
peg in place, the Mexican government had little choice but to offset the
increased demand by selling dollars and buying pesos to keep the value
stable. The more that Mexican consumers bought American goods, the
more dollars the Mexican government had to sell from its reserves to offset the imbalance.

By late 1994, just a year after NAFTA was passed, Mexico's dollar
reserves had dwindled from $29 billion to just $6 billion. In December,
the Mexican government announced it had no choice but to allow the peso
to float freely against the dollar. The peso plummeted. Within a matter of
months, the value of the peso had fallen by more than half. The price of
everyday products surged for Mexican consumers.

"The best that can be said about 1994," José Madariaga Lomelín, president of the Association of Mexican Bankers, said, "is that it is almost
over."

But 1995 wasn't any better. Inflation in Mexico surpassed 50 percent
by year end. The unemployment rate doubled. Interest rates soared, leading
to defaults on the adjustable-rate mortgages. Mexican companies fell even

farther behind their American competitors as their debt burden soared from the higher interest rates and a weak peso. Mexican banks suffered deep losses from their "can't lose" bets on interest rates.

The Mexican government again teetered on the verge of bankruptcy. Another rescue package was put together by the IMF, the US Treasury, the Federal Reserve, the Bank for International Settlements, and Goldman Sachs totaling $50 billion to keep the government afloat.

Rudi Dornbusch, a professor at MIT and a special advisor to the Mexican president, explained the Mexican crisis well: "The crisis takes a much longer time coming than you think, and then it happens much faster than you would have thought, and that's sort of exactly the Mexican story. It took forever and then it took a night."

Seeing an opportunity in the devalued peso and faltering government, American companies finally began putting their dollars to work. A shopping spree for discounted Mexican assets began for pennies on the dollar. The main winner was Walmart. In 1995, Walmart had eleven stores and more than twenty-two Sam's Clubs throughout Mexico. By the end of 1997, Walmart boasted fifty-six total locations.

Despite the NAFTA debacle, growth rates in other Latin America countries remained relatively strong in the 1990s. Economies in the region expanded at an average growth rate of nearly 5 percent per year from 1991 and 1997, a vast improvement over the "lost decade" of the 1980s.

Unfortunately, the growth stalled in 1998 as interest rates spiked throughout the region. Chile endured a painful recession, and Brazil required another IMF bailout. But it was Argentina that made headlines with an all-out economic collapse.

Like Mexico, Argentina had opted to peg its currency to the dollar to create stability in 1991. Initially, the move appeared to be effective; however, like most countries in the region, Argentina saw its economy begin to contract in 1998, leading to increased government deficits and debt. The recession morphed into a crisis by 2001: unemployment hit 20 percent, the government stopped paying workers, and the IMF refused to follow through on a pledge because of the massive government budget deficit. A run on the banks ensued, leading to a freeze on withdrawals. Argentine citizens were only allowed to withdraw minor sums, initially as low as $250 per week. Riots and protests erupted around the country.

Reeling from the crisis, Argentina was forced to abandon the currency peg with the dollar and default on nearly $130 billion of government debt. From 1999 to 2002, Argentina's economy contracted by an estimated 20 percent. At the depths of the crisis in 2002, nearly 70 percent of Argentinian children lived in poverty.

Following a brief surge of growth in the early part of the decade, Latin American countries experienced a strong contraction and deep recession during 2008–9. Emergency aid from United States and the IMF was again provided to various countries throughout the region.

Thankfully, China responded to the global slowdown in 2008 by increasing construction on a massive scale. China's construction boom, which will be discussed later in more detail, created a surge in commodity prices, which directly benefited commodity-rich economies in Latin America.

By 2010, China was South America's largest trading partner; the country increased shipments of virtually all major commodities, from soy beans to iron ore. In 2014, China accounted for more than 50 percent of the *global* consumption of cement, nickel, steel, copper, and coal. The consumption boom most notably impacted the larger South American exporters—Brazil, Argentina, Chile and Peru—and provided a welcome tailwind to growth throughout the region.

China's real estate boom eventually slowed, and commodity prices weakened, leading to a slowdown in many South American countries. Brazil and Chile both experienced recessions in 2015–16.

One positive trend that gives hope for improved stability in Latin American economies is the widespread realization that high inflation can devastate an economy. Most central bankers publicly embrace policies designed to target a predefined inflation rate. Mexico adopted inflation targeting in 2001 and saw the average inflation rate fall from 20 percent over the previous decade to 4 percent in the years since. Even in Brazil, the inflation rate has fallen to an average of 4 percent since 2006. The importance of price stability cannot be overstated for Latin America and provides long-term hope for a region fraught with economic uncertainty.

PART 3

Japan

15

THE RISE OF JAPANESE AUTOMAKERS

Ford knew people would be killed.

— *Juror, Grimshaw v. Ford Motor Company*

The following is the court summary from one of the many cases against the auto industry in the 1970s:

> In November 1971, the Grays purchased a new 1972 Pinto hatchback manufactured by Ford in October 1971. The Grays had trouble with the car from the outset. During the first few months of ownership, they had to return the car to the dealer for repairs a number of times. Their car problems included excessive gas and oil consumption, down shifting of the automatic transmission, lack of power, and occasional stalling. It was later learned that the stalling and excessive fuel consumption were caused by a heavy carburetor float.
>
> On May 28, 1972, Mrs. Gray, accompanied by 13-year-old Richard Grimshaw, set out in the Pinto from Anaheim for Barstow to meet Mr. Gray. The Pinto was then 6 months

old and had been driven approximately 3,000 miles. Mrs. Gray stopped in San Bernardino for gasoline, got back onto the freeway (Interstate 15) and proceeded toward her destination at 60-65 miles per hour. As she approached the Route 30 off-ramp where traffic was congested, she moved from the outer fast lane to the middle lane of the freeway. Shortly after this lane change, the Pinto suddenly stalled and coasted to a halt in the middle lane. It was later established that the carburetor float had become so saturated with gasoline that it suddenly sank, opening the float chamber and causing the engine to flood and stall. A car traveling immediately behind the Pinto was able to swerve and pass it but the driver of a 1962 Ford Galaxie was unable to avoid colliding with the Pinto. The Galaxie had been traveling from 50 to 55 miles per hour but before the impact had been braked to a speed of from 28 to 37 miles per hour.

At the moment of impact, the Pinto caught fire and its interior was engulfed in flames. According to plaintiffs' expert, the impact of the Galaxie had driven the Pinto's gas tank forward and caused it to be punctured by the flange or one of the bolts on the differential housing so that fuel sprayed from the punctured tank and entered the passenger compartment through gaps resulting from the separation of the rear wheel well sections from the floor pan. By the time the Pinto came to rest after the collision, both occupants had sustained serious burns. When they emerged from the vehicle, their clothing was almost completely burned off. Mrs. Gray died a few days later of congestive heart failure as a result of the burns. Grimshaw managed to survive but only through heroic medical measures.

Richard Grimshaw v. Ford Motor Company
119 Cal. App. 3d 757; 174 Cal. Rptr. 348

The jury deliberated for only a day and a half before reaching its decision: $125 million in punitive damages against Ford Motor Company, the largest judgment in US history at the time.

"The Pinto was the worst," said Mark Robinson Jr., an attorney for Grimshaw. "The tank was only 3 and 1/4 inches behind the differential housing, and in a crash the housing works like a can opener."

The design flaw made the Pinto highly susceptible to explosions in rear-end collisions. Worse yet, as the trial continued it became evident that Ford had known about the design flaw and the potential hazards but had chosen to ignore the problem in an effort to save money.

"Ford knew people would be killed," said one juror.

Ford's own records indicated that it could have provided the gas tank with extra protection in a collision for a mere ten to fifteen dollars a car.

"We came up with this high amount [of punitive damages] so that Ford wouldn't design cars this way again," recalled the jury foreman.

The punitive damages were later decreased to a mere $3.5 million after an appeal.

Six months after the Grimshaw case, Ford was on trial again. This time, the company itself was indicted on three counts of reckless homicide. The landmark case *Indiana v. Ford* marked the first time a corporation faced murder charges. In the case, which was remarkably similar to the Grimshaw case, a gas tank exploded after a rear-end collision of a 1973 Ford Pinto, killing three teenage girls.

Ford was ultimately found not guilty. Nevertheless, the cases marked a turning point for Ford's public image. In all, 117 lawsuits alleged damages from Ford's exploding Pinto.

Ford wasn't alone in its issues. General Motors received negative press over the Chevy Vega's rapidly rusting aluminum engine, as well as a false-advertising lawsuit over installing different engines in some of its Oldsmobile models. Chrysler's Plymouth Volare and Dodge Aspen experienced large recalls and become known for their poor quality. The struggling industry was ripe for a competitor to disrupt it, but no American companies appeared to be able to capitalize.

In July 1977, an interesting article appeared in the *American Machinist*, a trade journal for the machinery industry. The article, titled "Toyota's Famous Ohno System," introduced a new concept in efficiency creating a revolutionary advantage in Japanese automobile production.

Taiichi Ohno had worked as a former production engineer for Toyota Motors at end of World War II at a time when Toyota's productivity was noticeably lower than the big auto producers' in Detroit. Ohno saw an opportunity to compete by removing waste in the system and cutting down on inefficiencies thereby reducing inventory and storage costs. His system, referred to as the just-in-time method differed greatly from the American automobile industry, which was focused on quantity over quality, churning out parts and materials regardless of their usefulness.

"Normally you don't want workers or machines to be idle," Ohno explained when discussing the American approach, "so you keep on producing parts whether you need them at the assembly stage or not."

Rather than focus on sheer quantity of production, Ohno focused on quality, inventory control, and efficient use of labor, which in turn led to a dramatic cost advantage for the Japanese auto industry. By doing so, Toyota and Honda could earn a profit of $500 to $1,000 per car more than their American rivals. Equally important, the process improved quality, which meant less time in the shop and a lower total cost of ownership.

American auto makers used similar strategies during the 1940s but abandoned the approach with the explosion of demand from the Baby Boom generation. An American named W. Edward Deming is credited as a pioneer of the quality-over-quantity approach but was eventually rebuffed by the large US automakers as car sales increased. In July 1950, Deming was invited to give a speech to Japanese executives at the Industry Club of Japan in Tokyo. The executives embraced his ideas. In June 1951, less than a year after Deming's first lecture on quality control, Japan instituted the Deming Prize for industrial achievement. He continued speaking, coaching, and mentoring CEOs for the next four decades.

Increases in the price of gas, coupled with low-quality American models such as the Ford Pinto, brought Japanese innovation to the forefront of the automobile industry in the 1970s. Demand for smaller, more fuel-efficient cars increased rapidly, and Japanese imports to the United States rose fivefold to six million vehicles per year from 1970 to 1980.

The rise of Japanese imports was so sudden that concerned US automakers consistently pressured Congress to impose quotas and tariffs on the foreign automobile imports in hopes of offsetting Japan's cost advantage. In 1981, legislation was officially proposed to restrict Japanese imports in the name of protecting American auto workers. The proposal received broad support.

President Ronald Reagan, a proponent of free trade, worried that imposing tariffs on automobiles could have ripple effects throughout the trade relationship with Japan, but also felt that the tide of support was too great for him to override. Rather than fight back against the tariffs, Reagan and his staff encouraged Japan to issue quotas on its own auto industry to allow the American companies the time to retool and redesign.

"It takes 5, 6 or 7 years to retool to a completely new market demand. It would be appreciated if Japan would restrain [auto exports to the United States] for a limited period of time—3 or 4 years," former US trade representative William Brock reportedly told Japanese government officials.

The quota-vs.-tariff debate was more than just semantics. By self-imposing quotas on exports the Japanese automakers would reap the benefit of price increases arising from the supply/demand imbalance. A tariff, on the other hand, would have created a similar price increase from the additional tax, but the US government would have been the sole beneficiary.

Japan agreed and announced a self-imposed quota limiting imports to 1.68 million vehicles per year in May 1981. The decision allowed Japan to dictate the details of which cars were sold and how long the restrictions would last, but most importantly, heightened the demand for the limited supply. Japanese car manufacturers turned their focus from smaller, inexpensive cars to vehicles with the highest profit margin. The result was an inflow of luxury cars under brand names such as Lexus and Infiniti.

Technically, the self-imposed restriction lasted until 1994, but it was largely irrelevant years earlier as Japanese-owned car manufacturers like Toyota and Honda built factories and ramped up production within the United States to avoid the import quotas.

16

JAPAN BOOMS

He looked at me and said . . . "This is prime property."

— *Masao Nangaku's business associate*

Japan's increased market share in the US automobile industry was a mere microcosm of its emerging economic importance in the late 1970s and early 1980s. The country's technological innovations were quickly becoming the envy of the Western world, as evidenced by advancements in home entertainment and portable music. VCRs first became available in the United States in the late 1970s. The new technology allowed people to record a television program or watch a movie from the comfort of home. By 1985, 14 percent of American homes owned at least one VCR.

As an aside, a strong argument can be made that the industry caught on so quickly because unlike Sony's Betamax (the precursor to VHS tapes), VCRs allowed pornographic video. More than 75 percent of videocassettes sold were pornographic in nature in 1978 and 1979, pivotal years for the growth of the VCR industry. Three Japanese companies dominated the VCR market: Panasonic, JVC, and Sony.

Japanese innovation was also responsible for the explosion of the portable-music industry when Sony's cofounder asked the company president to devise some way for him to listen to music on the go—something small, portable, and lightweight, something he could use when walking around. In 1979, Sony released the Walkman, a fourteen-ounce cassette player with a leather case.

Sony's expectations for the Walkman were minimal: initial projections called for sales of five thousand units per month. Sony sold fifty thousand in each of the first two months, and the Walkman soon became a cultural phenomenon. Cassette sales boomed, surpassing vinyl for the first time in 1983.

American businesses scrambled to learn the secret of Japan's success. Books on Japanese management became best sellers with ominous titles like *Trading Places: How We Are Giving Our Future to Japan and How to Reclaim It*, and *Yen! Japan's New Financial Empire and Its Threat to America*. Harvard professor Ezra Vogel's book *Japan as Number One* described Japanese workers as the most efficient in the world and opened American eyes to other aspects of Japanese dominance, citing the infant-mortality rate as the lowest in the world and life expectancy as among the highest. Vogel's book was a bestseller for years in Japan.

Japanese dominance was a hot topic during the 1984 presidential election between incumbent Ronald Reagan and Democratic candidate Walter Mondale, the former vice president to Jimmy Carter.

"We have to stop following that white flag and start running up the American flag and turn and fight and make America number one again in international commerce so that American jobs are filled in this country," said Mondale. "What are our kids supposed to do? Sweep up around the Japanese computers?"

Reagan was criticized by many for his warm personal relationship with Japan's prime minister, Yasuhiro Nakasone. Their relationship, dubbed "Ron-Yasu" by the press, developed over mutual concerns about the Soviet Union during the Cold War. While ideal for diplomacy, many believed Reagan's friendship sheltered Japan from needed trade sanctions. Japan's trade surplus with America expanded from $9 billion to nearly $37 billion from 1979 to 1984 as Americans consumed more Japanese goods.

Nevertheless, Ronald Regan was re-elected. Ironically, despite his vocal concerns over Japanese trade, Walter Mondale would later spend significant time in Japan while serving as the US ambassador to Japan from 1993 to 1996.

Adding to Japan's competitive advantage in global trade, its currency, the yen, had remained relatively inexpensive compared to the US dollar. Government officials in America unofficially began accusing Japan of manipulating its currency. The weaker yen, they argued, was propelling Japanese companies to prosperity by making Japanese products appear less expensive than comparable goods produced by US companies.

In response, officials at the US Treasury organized a secret meeting on September 22, 1985, with representatives from the United States, Germany, France, the UK, and Japan at the Plaza Hotel in New York to discuss a plan to rebalance global trade by strengthening the yen. The plan called for each country to sell US dollars at once, out of the blue, on the open market. The action, they reasoned, would force the value of the dollar lower, thereby strengthening the other currencies; currency manipulation on the highest level.

Interestingly, Japanese officials agreed to the plan as well, despite the apparent goal of making Japan less competitive in global trade. The most logical reasons for Japan's compliance were that (1) Japan chose between the lesser of two evils (fearing that tariffs and trade embargos were imminent, which would have crippled exports), (2) the stronger yen would play well on the global stage to increase the prominence of the currency, (3) Japan saw the strengthening yen as a way to buy less expensive imports.

The agreement, known as the Plaza Accord, was implemented, and the dollar declined more than 50 percent against the yen in the two years that followed. The stronger yen was intended to make Japanese products more expensive on the global stage and thus rebalance global trade in favor of the attendees at the meeting. Officials, however, had miscalculated the variables. Despite the higher prices, Americans still had a healthy appetite for Japanese goods. Furthermore, Japanese companies had become huge consumers of raw materials used in the production of cars and electronics.

The stronger yen afforded the Japanese companies with the ability to spend fewer yen on the same amount of inputs needed in production.

In other words, an increase in the yen didn't automatically translate into higher prices and less competitive trade. In 1985, Japan had a $56 billion trade surplus. By 1987, the surplus had ballooned to $96 billion, the exact opposite effect the Plaza Accord was intended to have on global trade.

The strength in the yen also offered a unique opportunity to Japanese companies and investors. Prior to the Plaza Accord in 1985, a Japanese investor would have needed 200 million yen to buy a $1 million property in the United States. By 1987, the same Japanese investor needed only 100 million yen to buy the same property. Even though the price hadn't changed in dollars, the stronger yen allowed Japanese investors to buy foreign assets cheaper. Japanese companies and individual investors turned their focus to the United States and began scooping up assets indiscriminately with the stronger yen. Direct investment in other countries increased threefold in the two years following the Plaza Accord.

Again, the United States was concerned. For the second time in two years, an emergency meeting was called. On February 22, 1987, the same countries that orchestrated the Plaza Accord rendezvoused again, this time at the Louvre Museum in Paris. The group announced a new plan. The idea was to effectively undo everything they had done at the Plaza Hotel two years earlier. Instead of selling dollars, the countries would collectively begin buying dollars to stabilize the global flow of funds in another concerted effort to manipulate currency prices.

This time, however, the currency markets didn't respond as expected. Perhaps word got out. Perhaps forces had already been set in motion. Either way, the dollar actually weakened more despite the concerted effort to strengthen it. The Japanese yen rallied 20 percent against the dollar by year end, sending the Japanese shopping spree into overdrive.

Masao Nangaku was one of Japan's billionaires at the time, with holdings mostly concentrated on high-end entertainment and retail such as hotels, bowling allies, ski resorts, and golf courses. On his first visit to Las Vegas, Nangaku fell in love with the Dunes Hotel and Casino, a

1,200-room hotel and golf course on the Las Vegas Strip that had fallen on hard times and been forced into bankruptcy. He bid $157.5 million before his trip home to Japan.

"He looked at me and said . . . 'This is prime property,'" Nangaku's business associate said. "He's a very forward-looking person. He's always looking ahead."

Midtown Manhattan also became a key target for real estate acquisition. The Dai-Ichi Mutual Life Insurance Company took advantage of the strength in the yen to purchase a majority interest in the Citicorp Center, a fixture of the New York skyline, and a minority interest in Citicorp's building at 399 Park Avenue for $670 million. The sale came at a perfect time to help offset Citi's Latin American woes, providing Citi with a reportable gain of $450 million before tax. Japanese developers also purchased Exxon's midtown headquarters for $610 million, while Mobil agreed to sell its Manhattan office tower to a Japanese investment firm.

Interestingly, the real estate boom was carrying over to Japanese soil as well. Land prices in Tokyo reportedly increased by more than 50 percent in 1987, and more than 20 percent in 1988. Across the country, real estate prices were going parabolic. Valuations in Tokyo's highest-end market topped out at an incredible $130,000 per square foot, more than one hundred times the cost of premium real estate in Manhattan.

Japanese corporations reaped the benefits of real estate appreciation. The Mitsubishi Group, which includes brands such as Mitsubishi Motors and Mitsubishi Electric, had unrealized real estate gains of more than $70 billion by 1989. The real estate boom could be leveraged into actual capital, as Japanese banks were eager to loan money based on the appreciated values, rather than the cash flows of business operations.

Large real estate deals soon morphed into gigantic corporate deals. On September 25, 1989, Japanese electronics manufacturer Sony reached a deal to acquire Columbia Pictures Entertainment, including its subsidiary TriStar Pictures, for $4.8 billion. Sony's core business of VCRs and camcorders was believed to be complementary enough to Columbia's movie business that the two companies could mutually benefit from the union. The purchase price equated to twenty-seven dollars per share, more than double the twelve-dollar share price at the beginning of the year. Analysts scratched their heads at the premium.

A little more than a month later, Mitsubishi Estate Co. announced that it was taking a 51 percent interest in Rockefeller Group Inc. The deal included a total of fifteen million square feet of rental space, 388 elevators, thirty-five restaurants, an ice-skating rink, and Radio City Hall. The $868 million deal came just weeks before the lighting of the famous Christmas tree at Rockefeller Center.

"Money talks very loudly," said New Yorker Sumner Baye. "It's amazing. I wish we could keep it in American hands. I don't think it's very good to be selling everything to the Japanese."

"I'm disturbed like a lot of people," James Hesslin told a reporter on his way through the center. "We seem to be selling the country away. New York is like that, Los Angeles is like that. The Japanese are buying property all over."

The Japanese stock market, the Nikkei 225, was soaring as well, more than tripling from 1985 to 1989, at which time the value of Japanese stocks accounted for a staggering 45 percent of the world's entire stock value by market cap. The United States, by comparison, accounted for roughly 33 percent of the global value of stocks.

Martin Roth shared some amazing statistics in his book *Making Money in Japanese Stocks*. By June 1988, Japan boasted eight of the ten largest companies in the world. The value of Japanese telecom company Nippon Telegraph and Telephone was higher than that of IBM, Exxon, General Electric, AT&T, Ford Motor, General Motors, Merck, and Bellsouth combined.

The average price investors paid for stocks on the Tokyo Stock Exchange in 1989 topped sixty dollars per dollar of earnings. Roth wrote, "$10,000 invested in Japanese stocks in 1982 would by early 1989 have grown to around $100,000, thanks to the simultaneous skyrocketing of the Japanese stock market and the yen."

Income levels in Japan couldn't keep up with the torrid price increases of assets. By the start of the 1990s, home prices in Tokyo reached eighteen times the average worker's salary, up from eight times income just five years earlier. To put that into perspective, if that same ratio held true in America, a typical household with an income of $50,000 would be faced with home prices averaging $900,000. For practical purposes, Japanese real estate was unaffordable for almost everyone actually living in Japan.

The unexpected boom in real estate prices forced economists to justify the increases with theories of labor shortages and Japanese business dominance. In reality, the stellar performance of Japan's domestic real estate market and stock market had little to do with management styles or labor issues. The bubble in housing was easier to attribute to excessive credit growth and money creation fueled by a process known as "window guidance" orchestrated by Japan's central bank.

The Japanese central bank, aptly named the Bank of Japan, is responsible for interest rate policy, taking deposits, making loans to other banks, and issuing currency. Its responsibilities are similar to the Federal Reserve's, but the methods are quite different. Most notably, the Bank of Japan used a practice known as window guidance, in which the Bank of Japan made lending "recommendations" to banks. The recommendations were reportedly so detailed that they gave specific loan quotas for each sector of the economy as well as specific quotas for increasing lending. This allowed the Bank of Japan to control not only the money supply, but also which industries received loans. This process was designed to promote smooth economic growth throughout the economy.

The prescriptive approach worked beautifully for years, effectively creating an even distribution of economic growth. Unlike American companies, Japanese companies leaned heavily on bank loans to finance projects during the 1980s and 1990s. In contrast, in the United States, for instance, if General Motors decided to borrow $1 billion, the company likely wouldn't take out a loan from a bank. Rather, it would issue bonds through an investment bank and borrow money from the bond-buying public. In the Japanese system, corporate borrowing was done almost primarily through traditional banking; therefore, the window-guidance recommendations could dramatically accelerate or decelerate the economy in short order by increasing or decreasing the amount of money in circulation at any given time. This gave exceptional power to the Bank of Japan.

Furthermore, the guidance removed much of the burden of detailed credit analysis from the Japanese banks when analyzing potential borrowers. Inexplicably, however, despite the boom times of the late 1980s, the Bank of Japan continued setting remarkably high growth quotas for bank lending. In time, as the economy expanded, fewer productive projects could be found and lending shifted into less productive ventures such as real estate speculation. Regardless, bankers continued to increase lending to meet growth quotas.

17

JAPAN COLLAPSES

It's beginning to look like a nightmare.

— *Makoto Toda, Nippon Life Insurance*

"Ask any golfer around the world to name a golf course in the United States, and Pebble Beach will be the first thing they say," said golf legend Tom Watson, winner of the 1982 US Open at Pebble Beach.

Perched atop a ledge on the Pacific coast, Pebble Beach provides panoramic views of the ocean and is widely known as one of the more challenging courses in the country. In addition to the golf course, the Pebble Beach property consists of two hotels and hundreds of acres on the Monterey Peninsula. Perhaps the most distinctive attribute of the Pebble Beach course is that it is one of the few world-class golf courses that has remained open to the public since its inception.

Alan Shipnuck of *Sports Illustrated* wrote, "Pebble Beach is more than just America's greatest golf course, it's a national treasure. The beauty is unsurpassed and so is the drama created by so many thrilling, famous holes. No golfing life is complete until you've experienced Pebble's coastline, following in the footsteps of Nicklaus, Watson and Woods and an untold number of everyday dreamers."

In the fall of 1990, at the peak of Japanese speculation, a Japanese investment group bought the Pebble Beach property for more than $800 million. The purchase provoked an immediate and harsh response about foreign ownership of an American landmark. Critics grew even louder as rumors surfaced that the Japanese company planned to turn the course private and sell memberships, a technique that had become popular throughout Japan. The membership offered golfers two hours of preferred tee times each day for life for the price of $150,000. However, the California Coastal Commission refused to approve the plan.

"I bought the property not knowing how strongly the local community would object," said one Pebble Beach investor from Japan. Eventually the plan to sell private memberships was scrapped, and Pebble Beach was sold eighteen months later to another Japanese company at a loss of nearly $350 million.

The buyers of the revamped Dunes Hotel in Las Vegas weren't faring much better than the Pebble Beach investors. The hotel was losing half a million dollars a month. Analysts estimated the property value at $50 million less than the original purchase price. The inflated prices paid for American assets were taking their toll on Japanese investors.

"Anything that they bought is not worth what they paid for it," said Howard Sadowsky, an executive of a New York-based real estate firm.

"It's beginning to look like a nightmare," said Makoto Toda, director of the international planning department at Nippon Life Insurance in Tokyo.

Shortly after the Rockefeller Center purchase, rental rates in New York City began to decline. By 1992, Rockefeller Center was bleeding nearly $50 million a year in cash.

Sony too was experiencing large losses after purchasing Columbia Pictures for a dramatic premium. Escalating costs and box office flops began to take their toll on Sony's movie business. In November 1994, Sony announced a $2.7 billion write-off from its Columbia investment.

The losses were also painful in downtown Los Angeles, where Japanese investors owned roughly 45 percent of all premium commercial square footage, but Japanese investors weren't the only ones losing. The property slump was impacting American real estate moguls as well. In an ironic twist, real estate investor Donald Trump was forced to file Chapter 11 bankruptcy on four separate properties, including the Plaza Hotel, the meeting place for the Plaza Accord, which had played a pivotal role in inflating the real estate bubble initially.

"The Japanese were no dumber than the Americans," said Anthony Downs, a Brookings Institution real estate expert in Washington. The difference in Japan's case was the banks' easy access to credit. Unlike US banks, Japanese banks had loaned money based on the perceived value of the property while essentially ignoring the cash flow needed to pay interest. Furthermore, banking laws in Japan were far more lenient than US banking laws in determining how much could be lent.

No single reason explains why the bubble in real estate burst, but shortly before the Pebble Beach purchase, a new president named Yasushi Mieno had taken over at the Bank of Japan. Mieno was concerned that the Japanese economy was overheating, as evidenced by the soaring real estate prices, unsustainable debt loads, and lack of affordable housing in large cities. In an effort to slow the economy, the Bank of Japan increased interest rates. It also made the surprising decision in 1991 to cease the practice of window guidance altogether and allow bankers to decide for themselves which borrowers were worthy of loans. Unwilling and untrained to make the lending decisions on their own, borrowing ground to a halt. With the faucet of easy money turned off, air began to flow from the bubble.

Real estate prices were weak in America, but they were cascading in Japan. Japanese companies watched in horror as buyers disappeared and asset values tanked. For many corporations, the business strategy turned from speculation and greed to sheer survival as they scrambled to pay down debt with any free cash flow to avoid bankruptcy. Capital flowed back into banks at a record clip, triggering a dramatic contraction in the money supply. As spending decreased, the prices of everyday goods began to fall.

A similar situation arose in the United States during the early years of the Great Depression: When stock values and real estate prices collapsed, corporations shifted into survival mode. Individuals and institutions alike stopped borrowing and spending, and they began hoarding cash to repay debt. Defaults mounted as companies went bankrupt. Believing that easy money had created the bubble, the government and the Federal Reserve refused to step in and provide aid for fear they would stoke the fire that started the problem. In response, American officials did nothing in the early years of the Great Depression and allowed the monetary supply to contract further, only amplifying the problem. Individuals continued hoarding cash. Rumors of bank failures created a panic as depositors stood in lines for hours to receive fractions of their original deposits.

Now Japan was experiencing a similar problem.

Stock prices in Japan, having more than doubled over the previous six years, plummeted 60 percent during the summer of 1992 as economic growth ground to a halt. It was a double whammy for the banks. Unlike US banks, which are prohibited from taking ownership positions in their borrowers, Japanese banks routinely became large shareholders of companies that received their loans. The crossholding ownership added an extra layer of risk to the banks' balance sheets. In 1990, at the peak at the bubble, Japanese financial institutions owned a staggering 46 percent of all outstanding stock in Japan. The collapse in prices erased trillions of yen from the banks' balance sheets, effectively reducing the amount of money available to lend. Japanese policy makers watched the supply of yen in circulation fall by nearly a third.

The Bank of Japan opted to decrease interest rates to incentivize debt refinancing and borrowing, but the response was muted. Rates were lowered again, but to no avail. Interest rates fell from 6 percent to 2.5 percent over two years, but companies refused to borrow more, electing instead to continue paying down debt at a rapid rate.

Scrambling for ways to stop the bleeding, Japanese officials increased government spending to buoy the economy through the rough patch. Rather than focus on tangible public works projects like Roosevelt enacted during the Depression, Japan's Ministry of Finance began pumping money into Japanese stocks in hopes of boosting prices. The ministry accounted for one-third of all stock transactions in the spring of 1993. The Ministry of Finance also selectively changed the accounting laws so that banks could mask their balance sheet problems for a time.

Markets stabilized from the increased flow of money, but the economy remained relatively flat for the following two years and real estate prices continued to decline. Banks eventually mustered the courage to lend again, but much of their lending flowed right back into the failing real estate market. The collapse lasted so long and was so exaggerated that officials wondered whether a complete reboot of the banking system would be needed to avert a large-scale banking crisis.

"The aftermath of the bubble economy is pretty severe," said Yoku Takanaka, president of an investment-banking firm. "You can't put a Band-Aid on it. You need an operation. The Ministry of Finance is telling these banks, 'let's have an operation here and get it out of your system and move on.'"

Initial reports valued Japanese banks' nonperforming loans at $348 billion. A later government audit found that the number was closer to $425 billion. Behind closed doors, the estimate was closer to $1 trillion. Losses from the bad loans had also sowed the seeds for fraud, which appeared to be rampant throughout the banking system. Without action, the banks appeared to be on track to languish for decades.

18

JAPAN'S MALAISE

I'm exhausted. I've reached my limit.

— *Takayuki Kamoshida, Bank of Japan*

Jin Matsushita joined Yamaichi Securities as a teenager and worked his way up through the ranks, eventually becoming a full-fledged stock-broker. By the late 1980s, Matsushita had an income of more than $150,000 a year plus a bonus that could match his entire salary. He celebrated as the Nikkei 225, Japan's stock index, peaked near 39,000 in late 1989.

"It was a kind of miracle, I suppose," Matsushita recalled.

Like most Japanese workers, Matsushita was fiercely loyal to his employer. Unfortunately, Yamaichi Securities wouldn't survive the down-turn when executives got caught hiding losses. Matsushita had 90 percent of his life savings invested in the company's stock.

"My wife and I had furious squabbles over this after Yamaichi went down," he said quietly. "She asked how I could do this. But I worked for Yamaichi Securities," he explained. "It never occurred to me, never, that one day our company would not exist."

Time magazine ran a story on Matsushita:

> Sitting in the community room of a residential complex
> east of Tokyo, where he now lives, he explains how he
> bought his apartment in 1996, the year he retired from
> Yamaichi. He paid 76 million yen (about $775,000 at cur-
> rent exchange rates), borrowing 59 million yen of the total
> to finance it. That debt is the bane of Matsushita's exis-
> tence. When Yamaichi failed in 1998, wiping out most of
> his savings, he had no way to pay off the note with just
> his meager income from social security. The price of his
> apartment collapsed soon after he had bought it, so he
> can't sell. And unlike in the U.S., where owners can take
> their lumps and walk away from mortgages without the
> debt following them, Matsushita's is a "recourse" loan—
> common in Japan—which means that harsh penalties
> await those who fail to keep making payments for any
> reason.

Many in Japan found themselves in Matsushita's situation following Japan's
dramatic economic decline. In 1998, with no sign of recovery, Japan finally
began to address its banking mess. Not unrelated, the suicide rate jumped
34 percent in the same year. Sadly, suicide in Japan is a relatively common
occurrence.

The Aokigahara Forest, located at the base of Mount Fuji, is known
as the Suicide Forest. The forest is the result of a volcanic eruption over a
thousand years ago. Lava spewed from the volcano, covering miles around
the base of the mountain. Over the next several centuries, trees managed
to grow through the dried lava, creating a carpet of gnarled roots with
tightly packed coniferous evergreen trees. Cell phones and compasses routinely malfunction, a strange phenomenon blamed on the high concentra-
tion of iron in the dried lava covered over by a thin layer of soil. Travelers
report an eerie quietness throughout.

The forest has become Japan's number one destination for suicide. The unique solitude and eeriness coupled with pop culture references led the forest to become the second most common location in the world for suicides, trailing only the Golden Gate Bridge in San Francisco.

Signs and plaques are sprinkled throughout the forest with messages such as "Your life is a precious gift from your parents" and "Please consult the police before you decide to die!" Still, every year police and volunteers come together to walk the forest in search of bodies. The remains are collected to provide a proper burial. While the Japanese government stopped keeping statistics in the early 2000s, it is estimated that seventy to a hundred bodies are recovered from the twelve-square-mile forest each year.

Suicide is viewed differently in Japanese culture than in Western cultures. During the samurai period, suicide was viewed as an honorable method of dealing with defeat or failure. More recently, kamikaze bombers were celebrated for their heroic suicide. Unlike Christian culture, which views suicide as a sin, Japanese culture has spent centuries embracing suicide as an honorable way of removing oneself from a bad situation, despite the pain inflicted on loved ones.

In a twisted way, suicide can actually serve as a legitimate way to improve a family's financial standing in Japan. In America, the act of purposefully killing oneself generally exempts a life insurance company from having to pay a claim. In Japan, that's not the case. Japanese life insurers view suicide as an acceptable death claim, and they routinely pay out to the deceased's heirs. The majority of suicides in Japan are financially motivated. Statistics show that more than half of the deceased have historically been unemployed.

Following World War II, economic hardships in Japan led to an increased occurrence of suicide claims on life insurance contracts. This type of tragedy occurred so frequently that life insurance companies were finally forced to put a clause in their policies exempting them from paying a claim from death by suicide in the first twelve months of the policy. Still, many saw death as the only way out, and suicide rates routinely spiked in the thirteenth month. Through the years, the suicide clause has been challenged as a detriment to society. Regardless, the Japanese supreme court

IN LIGHT OF YESTERDAY 129

ruled that insurance companies "must pay for suicides" as long as the death doesn't violate preset terms in the contract.

Japanese finance laws don't typically allow for separation between business and personal assets. Individual business owners (and sometimes executives) are considered personally liable for the failure of their business. In many cases, loan collectors have even pressured the responsible party into suicide as the only alternative for repayment. There is a term for such a suicide in the Japanese culture: *inseki-jisatsu*, which roughly translates to "responsibility-driven suicide." Sadly, suicides also became commonplace within the leadership of Japanese banks trying to fix or hide their problems.

In September 1997, the Japanese Ministry of Finance announced that Japanese banks held $234 billion in nonperforming loans. A couple months later, the number was revised to $586 billion to include a broader definition of nonperforming loans. A final recalculation in the summer of 1998 brought the total to $880 billion. Seven years after the real estate meltdown, delinquent and worthless loans still accounted for more than 25 percent of the entire economy. Less than a decade earlier, Japanese bankers had appeared to be the best and brightest. Japan boasted the largest ten banks in the world at the end of the 1980s. By the late '90s, rumors of scandals, hush money, and organized crime filled the headlines in Japan. The horrendous debt burden had brought to light a variety of illicit activities such as giving guarantees to preferred investors, making huge loans for speculation in real estate and securities markets, creating shell companies for subsidiaries to hide bad loans from the bank balance sheets, and giving hush money to keep secrets from coming to light.

Government prosecutors raided one of Japan's largest and most well-known banks, Dai-Ichi Kangyo, in the summer of 1997 over allegations of ties to organized crime. A decade earlier, at the height of the Japanese mania, the bank had overtaken Citibank as the world's largest bank, boasting more than twenty million individual customers and having more than $200 billion in assets. Despite dwindling in size, Dai-Ichi Kangyo was still one of the country's more well-known banks. Officials seized documents and interviewed executives, eventually uncovering a long trend of fraudulent dealings involving hush money and under-the-table loans to organized-crime bosses dating back to 1989. The bank's former chairman, Kunji Miyaziki, killed himself in response to the allegations.

The scandals even extended to those in charge of the banking regulation. News surfaced that Japan's Ministry of Finance was turning a blind eye to the illicit practices, routinely giving advance warnings before "surprise" inspections and allowing the illegal activities to continue in return for lavish entertainment. In some cases, the Ministry of Finance reportedly offered advice on the best way to hide the activities.

Still reeling from the banking crisis, and upset over the fraud in the system, the public heaped blame on the Ministry of Finance as incompetent and corrupt. The Bank of Japan even joined in the finger pointing, as former executives publicly blamed the Ministry of Finance for the country's woes. In doing so, the Bank of Japan also made it clear that it would prefer to have full legal independence from the Ministry of Finance, which still serves as the regulatory body overseeing the Bank of Japan.

Public prosecutors raided Ministry of Finance offices in January 1998 and arrested two officials on bribery charges. The relatively minor charges consisted of favors totaling $20,000–$60,000 in return for lucrative government contracts and inside information from regulators. Still, the charges were enough to sway public opinion. The Ministry of Finance was relieved of its oversight duties of the Bank of Japan. Despite the Bank of Japan's role in causing the crisis with questionable window-guidance policies and loan quotas, it was now free from oversight.

In an effort to root out corruption and clean up its own image, the Bank of Japan announced plans to investigate its own internal policies. Takayuki Kamoshida, a thirty-five-year veteran of banking, was placed in charge of the investigation and tasked with punishing anyone involved in scandals within the Bank of Japan. He killed himself a month later.

"I'm exhausted. I've reached my limit," his suicide note read.

The headlines quickly shifted toward Long-Term Credit Bank, another Japanese megabank and the ninth-largest bank in the world (not to be confused with Long-Term Capital Management, the failed US hedge fund).

Long-Term Credit Bank had been extremely aggressive in lending to hotel acquisitions abroad, and reports began to leak that Long-Term Credit's loan portfolio was much worse than disclosed. The government decided to nationalize Long-Term Credit in October 1998. The shame was too much for Long-Term Credit Bank's corporate planning head, Takashi Uehara, who killed himself seven months later.

The government was also forced to nationalize Nippon Credit. Although unknown to most US investors, Nippon Credit was a household name in Japan. The bank had a similar-size asset base to Wells Fargo Bank, making it one of the fifty largest banks in the world at the time. Original estimates of Nippon's bad loans were $6 billion in the spring of 1998. Within six months, the estimate was raised to $15 billion. At the time of the government takeover at year end, news reports estimated non-performing loans at closer to $30 billion.

"This was an extremely sudden and regrettable move," said Shigeoki Togo, Nippon Credit's president. "Still, the Government may have decided we can't go on for 10 or 15 years carrying these bad loans, and nationalization may prove to be the fastest way of getting rid of them."

The government set aside more than $600 billion to use in bank recapitalization, takeovers, and bailouts.

"This is what people have been waiting for, the Japanese Government getting strong and tough with the banks. Welcome to the new Japan," said Robert Zielinski, head of Asian-bank research at Lehman Brothers.

Other analysts were less enthusiastic. "[Japan] is a loser's paradise, a country where inefficiencies are rewarded," said Jesper Koll, chief economist for Merrill Lynch Japan. "These zombie companies neither have good balance sheets nor operating performance. All they have is solid, old-style feudal lords who can get access to more revolving credit due to their political connections and their club memberships."

The insolvent banks were generally equipped with new management tasked with turning the bank around. In the case of Nippon Credit, the leader tapped to head the turnaround was Tadayo Honma, a sixty-year-old banking veteran who had formerly served as an official with Japan's central bank. Honma was named president of Nippon Bank on September 1,

2000. His tenure lasted two weeks before he committed suicide by hanging himself from a curtain rod on a business trip.

Bank fraud, suicides, and bad loans were making headlines, but the Bank of Japan had other concerns beyond banking. The economy wasn't improving, and prospects didn't look much better. Consumers weren't spending, banks weren't lending, and prices of everyday goods were stubbornly falling. The Bank of Japan again tried to stimulate the economy with government-bond purchases totaling 400 billion yen per month in 1998 and increasing over time to 1.2 trillion yen per month by 2002. The program, referred to as quantitative easing, was intended to increase the capital available for lending. To further its efforts, the Bank of Japan adopted a zero-interest-rate policy in February 1999 in a last-ditch effort to stimulate the economy. The response was muted. There was little more the Bank of Japan could do. Retail bank lending declined for the next four years while deflation persisted throughout the economy for the better part of the next decade.

The Great Recession of 2008–9, set off by the mortgage crisis in the US, only complicated the difficulties in Japan. Japanese exports plunged more than 16 percent, the largest decline in Japan's recorded history. Unlike the slowdown in the 1990s, Japanese companies were quick to lay off workers and reduce inventories.

"Japan has taken a disproportionate hit in the economic downturn. Japan's exports are concentrated in the very sectors that had been hit the most in the economic crisis, like cars and electronics," said Yasuo Yamamoto of Mizuho Research Institute.

At the height of the market panic in October 2008, the Japanese stock index, Nikkei 225, hit its lowest level in twenty-six years, down more than 75 percent from its peak. The Bank of Japan responded promptly with increased liquidity to banks, and various stimulus packages, including increased spending on health care, child care, and infrastructure projects. Total stimulus accounted for about 5 percent of the entire economy. Government deficits and borrowing increased in response because of a shortage of tax revenue.

The stimulus spending was not without critics. "Our infrastructure is impeccable. More public works would be a surplus to real need. It would not stimulate anything but the construction industry," said Takayoshi Igarashi, a professor of politics at Hosei University.

Economic growth resumed in 2010, but the economy remained burdened with increased public debt and soft exports from a strong yen. Further stimulus of $6 billion was enacted with a focus on job creation and social welfare, but the stimulus was too little too late for Japan to retain its position in the global economy. Japan's prolonged slump was enough to allow China to become the world's second-largest economy, a position held by Japan for the previous forty-two years.

Shinzo Abe was elected prime minister of Japan in 2012 on the platform of reviving the Japanese economy. His plan, creatively nicknamed Abenomics by the media, called for using three arrows to end Japan's slump: spending, tax cuts, and large-scale reform. Essentially, it would mean even more deficit spending from the government and increased asset purchases from the Bank of Japan, the same approach used by the United States following the financial crisis in 2008. Having already engaged in asset purchases and money printing many times over the previous years, the Bank of Japan unveiled a new form of QE known as QQE, short for quantitative and qualitative monetary easing, which called for the equivalent of a $1.4 trillion spending plan. Japanese stock prices rallied more than 50 percent in 2013 on the hopes that the economy would respond.

Yukio Noguchi, a professor of finance at Tokyo's Waseda University, cautioned that "without a revival of the real economy, this is all just voodoo economics."

Japanese stocks continued to rally through 2014, but true economic growth was elusive. The only effect from the stimulus appeared to be rising asset prices.

"The only people benefiting from this boom are foreign money managers and the rich," said Yuichi Magata, a taxi driver in Tokyo.

For decades, Japanese officials have tried to return the country to its glory days based on the assumption that sustained economic growth is still possible, but demographics no longer favor the aging country. In the wake of World War II, Japan's population had been young and well educated. In the 1950s, there were 11 working-age people for everyone over age sixty-five, which propelled Japan's economy to the second largest in the world. By 2013, the ratio was down to 2.5 working-age people for every person over age sixty-five. Even more concerning for Japan is that the country's workforce is actually shrinking. The population is aging so dramatically that the death rate now surpasses the birth rate. Regardless of the amount of stimulus, the unfavorable demographics make long-term economic growth much more of a challenge.

Still, the Bank of Japan has continued with the stimulus. A new stimulus plan calling for stock purchases by the central bank began in December 2015. Rather than choose select companies to invest in and risk playing favorites, the Bank of Japan began purchasing a basket of large Japanese stocks through the use of exchange-traded funds (ETFs). By April 2016, the Bank of Japan was a top-ten shareholder in 90 percent of publicly traded companies in Japan. While the stock market rally continued, the economy sat still. Government officials remained unclear on how the asset purchases would help the central bank reach its goal to grow the economy.

"The BOJ did not live up to expectations," said Norio Miyagawa, a senior economist at Mizuho Securities. "Increasing ETF purchases makes no contribution to achieving 2% inflation. The BOJ won't admit it, but it has reached the limits of quantitative easing and negative rates."

All the stimulus and spending has also increased Japan's debt burden. Total Japanese government debt in 1990 equaled 67 percent of the total size of the economy when the deflationary spiral began. By 2015, after years of budget deficits and stimulus spending, the debt load had ballooned to 250 percent, larger than in any developed country in recorded history. The only thing keeping the debt burden from crushing the country is two decades of interest rates near zero percent.

Japan's meteoric rise and subsequent collapse serves as a fascinating study in monetary policy mistakes. Living standards remain relatively high in Japan, poverty remains low, and Japanese companies are still among the world's leaders in technological innovation. Despite being overtaken by

China as the world's second-largest economy, Japan still enjoys a per capita income of roughly triple that of the Chinese.

At this point, returning to the glory days of sustained economic growth seems unlikely. Japanese leaders would likely be wise to adjust their monetary policy accordingly and discontinue the various stimulus measures rather than continually increasing the country's debt load. Japan's zero percent interest rates are no longer an outlier on the global stage. The inevitable future rate increases around the world will likely put increasing pressure on Japan's debt burden and the value of the yen. The transition won't be easy for policy makers.

PART 4

Europe

19

CREATION OF THE EURO

I want the unification of Europe because I promised it to my mother.

— *Helmut Kuhl, German Chancellor*

Every year in early May, countries in the European Union celebrate Europe Day, which highlights an agreement between West Germany and France to pool their coal and steel production in 1950. The pact was viewed as the first step back on the road to promote peace and unity throughout Europe following World War II. The deal eventually morphed into a formal free trade deal, the Treaty of Rome, which became the backbone of reconciliation for the continent. As years of peace continued, demand grew to unify European interests with a shared currency.

Fast forward to 1969. France was losing competitiveness in global trade. The franc had remained persistently weak, and the country spent a large portion of its foreign reserves to keep the currency pegged to the dollar. At the time, each European country's currency was restricted to a fixed exchange rate by the terms of the Bretton Woods Agreement, as discussed previously. For France, it appeared that the fixed exchange rate regime was beginning to unravel. Accordingly, France became the main driver behind the idea of a shared European currency following a series of embarrassing currency devaluations. Under the terms of the Bretton Woods Agreement, countries could request a devaluation to a new fixed rate with the approval of the IMF if economic forces demanded. The process, however, was tedious and politically unpopular as it implied economic inferiority.

A single-currency system would offer numerous economic benefits to European countries. There would be no need to change currencies when visiting each country, less currency risk for importing and exporting (leading to increased trade), and increased likelihood of continued peace throughout the region. The larger challenge would be forming the monetary union without a political union.

The United States is one example of the success of a single-currency system. The fifty states enjoy free trade and a uniform currency. While each state is free to set its own state tax rate, citizens are free to move from one state to another without the loss of federal government benefits such as Social Security, welfare, or Medicare.

The motivations behind the common European currency were not universally shared. Richer countries like Germany and the United Kingdom enjoyed the benefits of a strong currency and saw little economic benefit from giving up their home currency for a regional one. As the largest economy in Europe, Germany's involvement was critical to the success of a shared currency.

The Nixon shock in 1971 unexpectedly nullified the Bretton Woods Agreement and opened the door for a currency experiment in Europe. As a test run at a single currency, nine European countries agreed to fix their currencies loosely to one another. The cleverly named plan, "snake in a tunnel," allowed for intra-European currency fluctuations up and down within a tight range. Each country committed to buying and selling every other member country's currency on the open market to keep both currencies within the given bands. The plan would not only require constant oversight, but could also require depleting currency reserves in order to keep the relationships stable.

The challenge with any fixed currency regime is that interest rate fluctuations, trade imbalances, and government budgets each impact the value of a currency on a large scale. The United Kingdom quickly recognized the currency complications and left the "snake" after only one month. Germany's central bank president, Karl Klasen, shared his concerns about the outcome. "We are struggling to keep alive the snake in the tunnel," he said. Within a year Italy left the agreement as well, as did France.

The likelihood was diminishing that a common currency would work for so many different countries with diverse economies. European countries made a second attempt at fixing currencies in the late 1970s under a new name, the Exchange Rate Mechanism (ERM). Unfortunately, the results were similar. Inflation concerns and interest rate differentials complicated the efforts to keep currency values stable. France and Italy were both forced to devalue their currencies despite the targeted peg. Regardless, the idea of a common European currency was seen by many as the final barrier to free trade and continued peace.

British prime minister Margaret Thatcher, was critical of the single-currency system, voicing her concern that a common currency would hinder a country's ability to set tax policy and reduce its ability to recover from a crisis. She was, however, in favor of a common market, which didn't necessarily need a common currency. "I had one overriding goal. This was to create a common market," Thatcher wrote in her autobiography.

German chancellor Helmut Kohl initially shared Thatcher's view: "It (a common currency) poses a heap of problems for me, my majority is reluctant, the business community does not want it, the time is not right."

Public opinion in Germany was generally opposed to the adoption of a new currency. Economically, there was little reason for Germany to risk any economic disruption by implementing a large-scale currency change. The president of the German central bank, Karl Otto Pöhl, expressed deeper concern about the motivation for the common currency, claiming that France and Italy simply "wished to topple the (German) Deutschmark from its pre-eminent position."

Regardless, the leaders of the region held meetings and discussed policies, with France being the main driver behind the push for a common currency. For years, Germany's key decision-makers, including Kohl, were clearly opposed to the idea.

Unexpectedly, Chancellor Kohl's view changed in 1990, when he broke from the German consensus. Even though most Germans, including the central bank president, opposed the common currency, Kohl explained to US secretary of state James Baker that he had chosen to move forward with the plan because it was "politically important" to do so and because Germany "needs friends." On a deeper level, Kohl explained his motivation by saying, "I want the unification of Europe because I promised it to my mother." Like so many Europeans, Kohl had lost loved ones (his brother and uncle) during World War II and ultimately agreed that a common currency would help bring lasting peace to the region.

In 1992, officials met in the Netherlands and signed the Maastricht Treaty, which laid out the official framework behind the common currency to be known as the euro with an official launch date of January 1, 1999. German officials insisted that the key to making the plan work would be financial discipline among the member countries. While Kohl now approved of the common currency, he made it clear that he had no intention of offering German tax revenue to create a fiscal union within the region. Rules were established to restrict budget deficits and national debt levels for member countries.

Ultimately, the romance of peace and unity trumped the details behind the economic complexities of using a common currency for nineteen different countries with vastly differing economies. "Fundamentally, what clearly was a driving force was the fact that we had two World Wars," said the chairman of the Federal Reserve, Alan Greenspan. The creation of the euro "was a geopolitical decision with economic wrappings."

The details behind the economic wrappings were the challenge. The European Central Bank was established to set interest rates for the new monetary union and preside over the creation of the new currency. In doing so, interest rates in the member countries began to converge. Before the institution of the European Central Bank, consumers in each country borrowed at different interest rates relative to each country's prevailing rates. Likewise, the government of each respective country had different borrowing costs when issuing bonds. The advent of the euro normalized rates and made it possible (in theory) for countries like Italy and Spain to borrow and lend in the same manner as larger countries like Germany.

The convergence of interest rates led to lower rates in countries like Greece, Spain, and Ireland, which set off a boom in economic activity. Soon a housing bubble began to develop in southern Europe as banks in Portugal, Ireland, Greece, and Spain experienced credit growth increases of more 20 percent per year from 2004 to 2008.

"At the outset of the creation of the euro in 1999, it was expected that the southern Eurozone economies would behave like those in the north; the Italians would behave like the Germans. They didn't," said Greenspan.

For centuries, each European country operated as an independent entity, free to develop its own unique advantages and strengths and to increase and decrease interest rates as needed. Some countries relied heavily on manufacturing and exports. Others depended on imports and tourism. As each economy changed, so did the demand for one currency over another. As a country's economic prospects weakened, so too did the currency. The weaker currency led to less expensive exports and served to rebalance the country's competitiveness in global markets. With a unified currency, no such rebalancing mechanism existed and the imbalances grew. Unfortunately, by giving up control over its interest rates and monetary policy, each country also gave up some economic flexibility—the exact flexibility needed to fight a financial crisis like the one faced in 2008.

20

EUROPE IN CRISIS

The euro is like a bumblebee.

— *Mario Draghi, president of the European Central Bank*

As the banking crisis took root in the United States and made its way overseas, Europe found itself especially vulnerable. By 2008, the major US banks had locations in every corner of the developed world and had done a marvelous job spreading the subprime mortgages and derivatives across the global banking system. Analysts at the International Monetary Fund reported that European banks may have even had a higher overall allocation of the toxic mortgages than US banks.

As real estate prices collapsed around the world, construction jobs vanished and the unemployment rate in southern Europe soared. Government borrowing surged in Greece, Spain, Portugal, Italy, and other European countries as they tried to cope with a slumping economy. Short on tax revenue, government deficits rose past the levels set forth in the original agreement governing member countries.

One by one, European political leaders concocted similar quantitative-easing plans to inject billions of euros into their own banking system. Britain announced a £200 billion program. The French government decided to begin taking equity positions in the country's distressed banks, much like the US government had done for so many US banks. France also pledged 100 billion euros to plug the holes in its financial system. The Norwegian central bank agreed to provide the equivalent of $58 billion in additional liquidity to its banking system.

Even without the crisis in the US subprime-mortgage market, most economists believe that European banks would have eventually seen a day of reckoning from overleverage and a housing bubble in select countries. The US real estate debacle merely sped up the process. Regardless, throughout Europe, bad bank loans in the private sector were turning into bailouts from the public sector; tax revenue was being shoveled into the failing institutions.

In 1982, before *bailout* was a common term, Mexico faced a similar issue. As the crisis deepened, Mexico opted to nationalize a large portion of its banking system for similar reasons. Other countries throughout Latin America had been forced to follow suit. In doing so, however, the banking problems in Latin America morphed into government problems and ultimately became a currency problem. Now Europe was experiencing a similar issue.

With an economy roughly the size of the state of Washington, Greece became the poster child of Europe's problem. Greek citizens enjoyed much more generous pensions than other European countries despite having a younger average retirement age and much worse tax collection. Taxpayers there seem to pride themselves on tax avoidance. An IMF report found that the tax collected in the country routinely hovered around 50 percent of the tax revenue actually owed.

"Most small companies know they will never be audited so they don't bother to pay taxes," an unnamed European official said after being sent to assist in overhauling the Greek tax system.

A Greek senior government official offered the alternative take: "The Greek economy would collapse if the government were to force these people to pay taxes."

As tax collection fell and pensions rose, the federal deficit in Greece increased each year. Soon Greece was primarily funding its liabilities with borrowed money. Still, for years, banks and investors had chosen to look past Greece's issues, on the belief that "countries don't go broke." With Greece buoyed by the common currency, the loans continued.

The economic downturn from 2007 to 2009 struck a direct blow to the Greek economy. Unlike the rest of the world, European countries had fewer options to fight the crisis because the euro agreement imposed budget constraints. Government budget deficits in Greece were already four times larger than the highest threshold allowed. Prime Minister George Papandreou imposed austerity measures—spending cuts and government layoffs— and attempted to increase taxes. The problems only worsened. Unable to jumpstart the economy, Greece accepted a joint bailout from the European Central Bank, the International Monetary Fund, and the European Commission of $143 billion in 2010 and another bailout of $170 billion in 2012.

As in Latin America three decades earlier, the loans kept the poorer country afloat but the austerity measures caused the people great suffering. Unemployment hit 25 percent, and more than 60 percent of Greek children lived in poverty. Greek stocks fell 90 percent from the peak. At its low point, the entire stock market was worth less than the American discount retailer Costco.

Pressure grew throughout the Eurozone that the region might need to abandon the single currency. Rumors surfaced that the Germans wanted out, too. Many questioned how long the richer countries would be willing to continue funding and bailing out poorer countries with weak fiscal restraint like Greece.

In the United States, prolonged economic slumps in one state can be overcome by workers simply moving to another state to find new opportunity. In Europe, the mobility of labor is less viable. Moving from one country to another for employment is more complicated, and generally means restarting government benefits in the new country. Without a fiscal union in Europe, each country has its own method of calculating benefits and differing age restrictions. US citizens, on the other hand, are assured of the continuity of government programs such Social Security,

Medicare, disability and unemployment coverage regardless of which state they reside in.

By 2012, the crisis had largely run its course in America. Consumer confidence had returned, and with it, consumer spending increased. Much of the credit for the US recovery was attributed to the policies of the Federal Reserve led by Ben Bernanke. Europe, however, wasn't having a similar experience. Thankfully, Europe had its own version of Ben Bernanke in the person of Mario Draghi.

Draghi was tasked with heading the European Central Bank in 2011. He was well spoken, well connected, and well respected, but he had an extra level of stress beyond that of Bernanke. The European Central Bank was the primary link holding the European region together. With no central European government to rely on for fiscal support, Draghi was the closest thing to a unifying player in all of Europe, and investors were beginning to lose faith in the euro experiment. Despite record-low interest rates, some countries in the Eurozone were having to pay investors far more than neighboring countries to borrow money. In Portugal, short-term interest rates on government bonds approached 20 percent. In Greece, the rate eclipsed 40 percent.

Europe's big currency experiment appeared to be on the cusp of failure. Tensions ran high, and analysts were calling for the exit of Greece from the euro. In speech after speech, Mario Draghi had tried to reassure the world that the European Central Bank would continue to be accommodative with monetary policy. In the summer of 2012, Draghi tried a new tact. He stepped to the podium at a conference in London and began talking about bumblebees.

"The euro is like a bumblebee," Draghi began. "This is a mystery of nature because it shouldn't fly but instead it does."

Draghi didn't elaborate on the science behind his statement—that bumblebees' bodies are too large relative to their wing size or that bumblebees seem to defy the laws of physics—but his message was clear. Draghi didn't elaborate on how he planned to the keep the bumblebee in the air, but he did emphasize one point: the bumblebee would remain in flight.

"Within our mandate," Draghi continued, "the ECB is ready to do whatever it takes to preserve the euro. And believe me, it will be enough."

Draghi's tone oozed with confidence. And it needed to. He was trying to convince five hundred million people living in the European Union and government leaders from each of the nineteen countries that the euro would persist. Ironically, Draghi's words worked better than any action he had taken up to that point. Having previously provided over a $1 trillion in aid with little response, Draghi's words carried weight. News outlets grabbed onto the statement.

Interest rates in the southern countries of Europe began to fall back to more normal levels by the end of 2012. Draghi hadn't actually done anything in regards to policy, but his confidence and assurance had calmed investors. In time, the speech would become famous. The *Financial Times*, a London-based publication, named Draghi its person of the year, specifically citing his "whatever it takes" speech. The crisis began to subside, but economic growth remained stubbornly anemic. The time soon came for Draghi to take real action.

Draghi was subdued, almost nonchalant as he spoke. The move was expected. "The rate on the deposit facility was lowered by ten basis points to −0.10 percent. The negative rate will also apply to reserve holdings in excess of the minimum reserve requirements," said Mario Draghi in June 2014. There were no gasps from the crowd; no shock and awe came from the attendees of the press conference. Journalists quietly scribbled notes. Few made eye contact with each other. Nevertheless, the statement was monumental.

Debt levels throughout Europe had continued to grow as each country tried to stimulate growth. The results had been disappointing. The main fear throughout Europe was that deflation would take hold in the same way it did in Japan throughout the 1990s and 2000s. To fight deflation, the European Central Bank had to encourage consumer spending. Negative interest rates were the European Central Bank's economic Hail Mary. Draghi hoped that imposing negative interest rates would incentivize spending and borrowing by punishing savers. The negative interest rates didn't just apply to consumers. They would also apply to any idle cash the banks opted to hold in reserve with the European Central Bank. The belief was that the negative rates would make banks more apt to extend loans rather than hold cash.

Each major European bank holds reserves with the European Central Bank. This money is available to be lent out as needed through ordinary banking channels, but remains held at the central bank until requested by lenders. The banks are generally credited interest on the deposits as long as the money sits with the central bank. By imposing negative interest rates, the European Central Bank would be deducting money from the banks rather than crediting them. In essence, European banks would begin being penalized for not making loans.

It didn't take long for the negative interest rates to filter through the system. Within six months, the yield on five-year government bonds in Germany and Finland fell into negative territory, as did all government bonds up to seven years' duration in Switzerland. Yields on two-year government bonds in France, the Netherlands, Belgium, Austria, and Denmark also began trading with a negative yield.

For some, the negative rates were a welcome surprise. Hans Christensen, a financial consultant living in Denmark, had refinanced his home years earlier with a floating rate mortgage having no idea that interest rates could actually turn negative. In January 2016, Christensen opened his mortgage statement to find that the interest rate on his home had floated to a negative 0.0562 percent. Christensen still had to make principal payments, but the bank was actually crediting him the equivalent of thirty-eight dollars each month.

"My parents said I should frame it, to prove to coming generations that this ever happened," said Christensen.

"If you had said this would happen a few years ago, you would have been considered out of your mind," said Torben Andersen, a professor at Denmark's Aarhus University.

Even before the bank began paying him, Christensen was already taking full advantage of the ridiculously low rates. Two years earlier, he joined a small group of investors and purchased ten apartment units for $1.5 million, borrowing roughly $1.25 million of the total. The low interest rates were rekindling a fire in the Danish housing market.

"People feel that they have to use the money because it is so cheap," said Michael Soebygge of Nordjyske Bank.

Famed investor Warren Buffett shared his thoughts: "It does have the effect of making all assets more valuable." Buffett said, "I mean, interest rates are like gravity on valuations. If interest rates are nothing, values (on other assets) can be almost infinite. If interest rates are extremely high, that's a huge gravitational pull on values, and we had that in the early 1980s."

In the years that followed, Europe's economy muddled along with muted growth while financial markets remained surprisingly unresponsive. Debt levels have remained elevated, and interest rates remain negative in many parts of Europe. The long-term feasibility of the euro is still debatable, although tensions have subsided. In July 2016, a new reason for concern developed. Britain, having never adopted the euro as its home currency, made the surprising decision to exit the free trade region of the Eurozone. The details are still being debated, but doing so poses a host of risks to the region as trade deals will need to be rewritten and economic stability is threatened.

There is no clear path ahead for Europe. Complications persist with the common currency. Inflation and unemployment remain stubbornly high in parts of Europe, and concern is growing about the mounting debt burden in southern Europe.

PART 5

China

21

CHINA OPENS UP

But here the land is very cheap, so they save money.

— *Zhou Ganceng, factory manager*

For centuries, China's economy functioned primarily as a closed circuit; rarely engaging in global trade or allowing investment from the outside world. As such, China remained relatively poor, and the standard of living remained stagnant. That all changed in the late 1970s when an experimental economic policy fueled exponential growth and set the country on a new path to prosperity.

Deng Xiaoping rose to importance as a member of the Chinese Communist Party. He was a loyal confidant to the legendary Mao Zedong, revered leader in China throughout the bulk of the twentieth century. Deng originally earned praise for the way he handled a land-reform program in 1951 in which he confiscated land to be redistributed at the discretion of the Chinese government. He received much of the credit for the program's "success" despite the reported deaths of an estimated two to three million Chinese who were killed resisting the land confiscation.

A second, larger-scale land-reform movement took place in the latter part of the decade as Chinese leaders pushed to remake the Chinese economy by increasing the country's industrial prowess and agriculture. Known as the Great Leap Forward, from 1958 to 1961 an estimated seven hundred million people—more than double the present-day population of the United States—had personal property and land confiscated for government use. The people were then divided into roughly twenty-six thousand different groups known as communes, which consisted of five thousand to twenty thousand households that shared resources.

The primary task for working-age males within each commune was steel production, which became Mao's benchmark for industrial might and something of an obsession. Mao made it clear that he planned for China to surpass the steel production in the United States within the decade. Backyard furnaces were used by the communes to melt down everything from spoons, to shovels, to bicycles in order to increase steel production. The steel, however, was of low quality and generally inferior than that found elsewhere in the world, rendering it virtually unusable.

Within a year, food production was inadequate to support the communes as agricultural workers focused on producing steel rather than farming. It is estimated that twenty to thirty million people starved to death, although detailed statistics were not kept. Sadly, reports later found that more than twenty million tons of grain were being held by the government to be exported abroad at the height of the famine. Deng Xiaoping was at the heart of the disaster. Frank Dikötter, in his book *Mao's Great Famine*, blames Deng specifically for ordering the extraction of grain from starving peasants despite the domestic need.

For years, Chinese officials clung to the belief that economic advancement could be achieved through forced labor and social engineering. Despite the obvious errors in logic during the Great Leap Forward, industrial prowess remained the focus of the economy. Intellectuals, on the other hand, were viewed as dangerous. Education and intellect, Chinese officials believed, could sow the seeds for a disruption of the order. At one point, Deng had been tasked with leading an attack on Chinese intellectuals, which led to half a million citizens being sent to labor camps.

Despite the atrocities, Deng rose and fell in political power numerous times over the next fifteen years. His final triumphant return coincided with Mao Zedong's death in 1976, at which time Deng moved into the spotlight as a prevailing Chinese leader. At the time, China's neighbors were enjoying a significant level of economic advancement. South Korea, Taiwan, Hong Kong, Singapore, and, of course, Japan were becoming engines of economic growth in Asia. Meanwhile, China's economy had been stagnant for years.

By the mid-1970s, Deng had come to the startling and controversial realization that China's international isolation and lack of education were stunting economic development. He worried that regulations and restrictions put in place to protect the country might be the main forces limiting growth. Perhaps by loosening the reins he could stimulate economic development. In a search for inspiration, Deng began organizing trips abroad for Chinese officials to study other economies. From January to November 1978, the Chinese government sent more than five hundred different groups of researchers overseas to study the economies of other countries. In total, more than three thousand Chinese officials traveled abroad in search of ideas.

China's vice premier and third-highest ranking official, Gu Mu, was one of the selected travelers. Mu led various expeditions to Western Europe with Chinese specialists from different economic sectors personally visiting France, West Germany, Switzerland, Denmark, and Belgium in the summer of 1978. Mu and his specialists were amazed at the level of automation and the use of computers in Europe. The gap in technology compared to China was enormous, as was the overall level of economic development.

By the time of his return, Gu Mu reached the same conclusion as Deng: China needed to relax restrictions on foreign investment and begin trading with the rest of the world. Mu made his pitch to the other top Chinese leaders. He shared his conversations with the leaders of the European countries about their willingness to supply credit, export technology, invest directly in China, and even enter into agreements to import Chinese goods and services. His enthusiasm was infectious.

Surrounding countries had reached similar conclusions and enjoyed rapid economic growth. Taiwan embraced global trade more than a decade earlier by establishing the city of Kaohsiung as an official export-processing zone with semi-capitalist laws. The experiment had been a major success. South Korea experienced similar results with its first export zone in Masan in 1974. Again, the strategy proved wildly successful in the introduction of new technologies and the training of workers. Both countries' exports were thriving, which was having ripple effects on employment and economic development.

Taiwan and South Korea were notable examples, but it was Singapore, more than any other country, that offered concrete proof of the potential success an open economy could bring. The Singapore model allowed for a semi-capitalist system to exist alongside an authoritative regime.

"Singapore enjoys good social order and is well managed," Deng said at the conclusion of his personal visit in 1978. "We should tap their experience and learn how to manage better than them."

Eventually, China made the commitment to test the idea by opening four areas known as special economic zones. Rather than use established cities, China strategically selected four peripheral locations that could easily be forgotten if the experiment failed. Each zone was strategically located relatively close to a larger city, like Hong Kong or Macau, in an effort to attract migrant workers to the new cities.

Deng realized that to fulfill their full potential, these zones would need to become model cities, complete with diversified industries such as shopping and real estate development. To do so, the zones would be given different laws than the rest of the country, including preferential tax treatment to attract foreign investment. The first zone in Deng's experiment would be a small fishing village near Hong Kong known as Shenzhen, home to just thirty thousand inhabitants. At the time, the village's notable industries included primarily rice paddies and duck farms.

A sixty-seven-mile-long barbed-wire fence was constructed to circumscribe the economic activity. Chinese citizens wishing to work would pass through customs as if entering another country. Businesses in Shenzhen were not allowed to purchase land but were allowed to rent it at costs ranging from fifty cents to ten dollars per square foot depending on location and business use. At 15 percent, taxes were levied at only half the rate of the other areas in China. Workers, however, were hit with an additional 30 percent tax on all wages.

The majority of the early investment came from Chinese and Hong Kong businesspeople living abroad in need of relatively simple operations for assembling such products as radio recorders, electronic watches, handbags, and Cabbage Patch Kids dolls. Only $1.5 billion of investment in new factories flowed into Shenzhen, still, it was a massive amount of money for an area with virtually no previous development. Roughly 70 percent of the investment came in the form of assembly line operations. China was at the opposite end of the innovation spectrum from Japan. The country's exports were initially low-tech goods requiring minimal education and training.

Zhou Ganceng was the deputy manager of a factory making transistor radios that would eventually be exported to New Jersey. "The radio is simple. They could make it anywhere," he said, "but here the land is very cheap, so they save money."

The Western world was slower to embrace the changes in China. The only notable Western investments in the early years came in the form of a $20 million project by a small US company building and leasing oil-drilling rigs, and a $5.5 million Pepsi bottling plant. Despite making headlines with the move, the Pepsi plant only provided employment to thirty-five people. Wages at the plant began at roughly $100 per month—low by US standards, but nearly triple the monthly wage earned by the average Chinese industrial worker.

Lim Mon Foo was a marketing manager for Pepsi at the time. "From the beginning," she said, "they didn't know what to do, but when we trained them, they picked it up fast. Of course, there are a few who need some more supervision, but they can keep up."

Eventually workers began flocking to Shenzhen. The population tripled in the first four years to ninety thousand. Wages rose dramatically in the early 1980s, approaching an average of $100 per month for the average worker. DuPont, Pepsi, IBM, and Compaq each opened factories. KFC, Pizza Hut, and McDonald's entered Shenzhen as well. The meals cost a small fortune relative to the income of the average worker in China. Still, for many, the experience was worth the price, and locals flocked there to get a taste of America.

"What chance do I have to go to the United States?" Wang Yonglu, an elderly McDonald's customer said. "This way, I can spend only 10 yuan [$1.75] to see what America is like."

Chinese officials even chose Shenzhen as one of four locations for the country's major stock exchanges. Early estimates by city officials calculated expected population growth to hit four hundred thousand by 1990.

The success of special economic zones like Shenzhen led to further expansion of unique zoning areas. In 1984, authorities introduced smaller versions of special economic zones known as economic- and technological-development zones. Forty-nine such zones were established over the next eight years, as was one larger special economic zone. For an economy that had been relatively closed off to the rest of the world, China was quickly re-inventing itself as an export-driven economy.

"To become rich is glorious," Deng Xiaoping said in 1992 after touring various special economic zones. The sentiment in China was changing as the country began to embrace a more capitalist economy. Still, the country was far from rich. In order to become so, China would need to continue producing products and increasing exports at a rapid clip. This would require a dramatic increase in the sheer quantity of raw materials.

Geographically, China is blessed with a vast array of natural resources. The country is among the world's leading producers of coal, gold, aluminum, steel, rare earth metals, zinc, and iron ore. Regardless, the resources within the country were inadequate to fully supply the country based on the size of the population and scale of the growth in the overall economy. Vast quantities of resources would still need to be imported from other countries. Commodity imports grew twenty-fold from 1984 to 2004.

Within China, the companies tasked with extracting the natural resources through mining and oil production are state-owned enterprises controlled by the Chinese government. As demand grew for more commodities, so did the pressure to supply more. For years, the state-owned behemoths in China operated with the skill and grace one would associate with a clunky bureaucratic monopoly, but in the mid-1990s China began to grant more autonomy and allow each company to seek ways to maximize profit and diversify its economic footprint beyond China's borders. In 1999, China officially launched a new initiative, known as the Going Global Strategy, that encouraged overseas investment and cooperation with foreign companies. Rather than simply buying raw materials, these state-owned enterprises altered their strategy to begin partnering with or taking over foreign companies involved in the production of minerals, fossil fuels, commodities, and timber from resource-rich countries in Latin America and Africa.

Africa is the richest continent in terms of natural resources, with roughly 30 percent of global mineral reserves. In return for mineral rights, China invested heavily in Africa, undertaking large-scale projects like roads, railways, and dams. Soon, Chinese state-owned enterprises had become major players in the global mining industry, accounting for almost 15 percent of the global production of metals. China became the world's number one consumer of aluminum, copper, lead, nickel, zinc, iron ore, tin, steel, coal, cotton, and rubber consumption. Accordingly, China's total investment in Africa rose tenfold from 2005 to 2011. As a by-product of China's increased appetite for natural resources, commodity prices soared around the world.

Meanwhile, back in China, real estate prices were spiking as well, as the average home price tripled from 2005 to 2011. Real estate development boomed—perhaps too much, in that the number of vacant apartments surpassed 60 million.

22

CHINA'S CREDIT BOOM

They haven't even built a proper road here.

— Li Chun, car mechanic

The mortgage crisis in the United States sent shockwaves of a different kind through the Chinese economy. The banking system in China was one of the few to largely avoid the toxic-loan game. As state-owned enterprises, Chinese banks focused primarily on domestic financing and rarely ventured into holdings outside of the country. By the end of 2009, Chinese officials were confident that the country had avoided the full brunt of the crisis, as China boasted one of the few economies in the world that continued to post strong economic numbers.

However, as consumers around the world slowed their consumption of goods, Chinese exporters felt the pain. Officials feared that the global recession would create an employment crisis because of layoffs. In order to avoid such a spike in unemployment, China would need to replace the lost jobs in the manufacturing industry with jobs in another industry.

Unlike democratic countries, China has a unique advantage when dealing with a crisis. Government officials can stimulate the economy without manipulating interest rates or incentivizing the private sector to spend.

Rather, state-owned banks can increase loans on command at the request of government officials. Finding economically viable projects in need of financing is another matter. Nevertheless, Chinese officials determined that the best course of action was to increase investment in construction and real estate development.

To carry out the plan, city governments were instructed to confiscate land and auction it off for real estate development. In practice, land was generally acquired by simply taking over older neighborhoods and relocating the inhabitants to other areas involuntarily. In some cases, reparations were made. Nevertheless, land auctions soon became a primary source of revenue for local governments throughout China, generating more than $230 billion in 2009. In most cases, the land would be sold to a state-owned business paying a premium price. A study published by the National Bureau of Economic Research found that state-owned enterprises "paid 27% more than other bidders for an otherwise equivalent piece of land."

To finance the purchases, state-owned banks lent $1.4 trillion toward land purchases in 2009, double the previous year. Land prices soared as the strategy played out. Individual investors followed suit and scooped up investment properties. Home prices in Shanghai, Beijing, and Shenzhen increased more than 50 percent in 2009.

"People are using real estate as an investment, as a place to store cash; they treat it like gold," said Patrick Chovanec, a professor and leading expert on China's real estate market. "They're stockpiling empty units. This is going on in cities of virtually every size."

In 2010, more than eight hundred million square feet of real estate were bought and sold in China, more than in every other country in the world combined. Home prices continued to soar as investors bid up typical apartments to unrealistic prices. In Shanghai, home prices exceeded $200,000 despite average income throughout the city of only about $4,000 a year. China had avoided a slowdown in the global economy by creating a real estate bubble.

Eager to cash in on the surging prices, companies with no connection to real estate development began expanding their corporate footprints. The China Railway Group announced plans to develop residential apartments in Beijing. As the name implies, the China Railway Group engineered rail-roads, not residential construction. Likewise, the China Ordnance Group, a military supplier, expanded into real estate development with luxury resi-dences and retail outlets. Sino Ocean, a shipbuilder, paid more than $1 bil-lion for land to develop residential property in Beijing as well. The Anhui Salt Industry Corporation, a state-owned enterprise specializing in mining government-owned salt mines, branched out into luxury high-rise con-struction. Pressured by the government to show ever-expanding growth, state-owned companies borrowed huge sums of money from state-owned banks to buy state-owned land from local governments.

"These are the ones that have the money to buy the land," says Deng Yongheng, a professor at the National University in Singapore. "Because in China, it's the government that controls the money supply and the spending."

Chinese officials, well aware of the real estate bubble, decided to clamp down on excessive credit growth in 2010 by placing restrictions on bank lending to real estate developers, and on mortgages to individuals buying a third home in Beijing, Shanghai, or Shenzhen. The state-owned banks, subject to government demands, generally complied. The action should have been enough to slow the insanity, but it wasn't. Local government officials were still under great pressure to create growth at any cost. If they were unable to show economic growth, then Chinese officials in the national government would replace the local government officials with those who could. And this is where things get complicated.

With borrowing from state-owned banks limited, a new subsector of lenders emerged known as "shadow banks." These lending institutions were willing to make loans outside of the usual framework of state-owned banks. They weren't structured as banks; they generally didn't even take deposits or offer banking services. In most cases they merely served as pass-through entities. Through a variety of off–balance sheet methods, state-owned banks would extend loans to shadow banks, which would immediately extend the same loan to the real estate developers at a slightly higher interest rate.

To understand shadow banking in simple terms, let's assume company A can't get a loan but works out an arrangement for company B in a different industry to borrow money instead. Company B then extends the same loan to company A at a higher interest rate. In this example, company B represents the shadow-banking industry. These new black-market loans allowed borrowers to circumvent the restrictions placed on state-owned banks. The trick was to make sure the new loans were made by unregulated financial institutions outside of state control.

Shadow banks operated side-by-side with the large state-owned banks, which they had no intention of competing with. In fact, they were embraced by the traditional banks to fill the lending void caused by the banking restrictions. State-owned banks were also still under pressure to show profits, and in many cases still wished to make the restricted loans. The real estate development binge continued.

Official numbers show that bank loans to the real estate sector peaked in 2010 and were 40 percent lower by 2012. Unofficially, however, the lending continued to expand. In many cases, the shadow-bank loans were even packaged and sold right back to the larger state-owned banks. To show a quick profit, the state-owned banks would repackage and sell the repurchased loans to investors as "wealth-management products," which were an immediate hit with retail investors.

With limited investment options, most Chinese investors are left to choose between low-yielding bank deposits, select Chinese equities, real estate, and foreign currencies. Wealth-management products offer the possibility of a substantially higher return than traditional bank investments and fill a much-needed void in the average Chinese asset allocation. These wealth-management products were (and still are) widely perceived as providing the same safe protection as bank deposits despite the questionable nature of the underlying collateral.

Golden Elephant No. 38 was a wealth-management product highlighted by the *New York Times*; offering investors a 7.2 percent return, more than double the comparable return on a savings account in China. But what were investors actually investing in? The collateral backing Golden

Elephant No. 38 was described as "a near-empty housing project in the rural town of Taihe at the end of a dirt path amid rice fields in one of the poorest provinces in China."

"They haven't even built a proper road here," said Li Chun, a car repairman, and one of the few residents living in the project.

The wealth-management products being peddled by banks bear striking similarities to the AAA-rated pools of subprime mortgages that in 2008 nearly crashed the US banking system, in which pools of low-quality loans were repackaged and sold back to the unsuspecting public.

"In our view, this is not fundamentally different from a Ponzi scheme," said David Cui, a strategist with Bank of America.

Nevertheless, the public appetite for the loans allowed the game to continue and real estate development to expand. Soon, stories began making headlines in Western news outlets of complete towns built without any occupants. These ghost towns drew the attention of documentary film makers Song Ting and Adam Smith, who chose a near-empty town called Ordos as the focus of a 2013 film. At the time of their filming, the town had only thirty thousand residents despite infrastructure to support three hundred thousand.

"When we visited Ordos, most of the people we saw were seniors old enough not to have a job anymore. Some mid-aged farmers are still trying to work, but jobs they can find are either cleaning or physical labor work," said Song Ting. "Now they're trying to attract more big factories so these farmers can have jobs."

"On the empty highway surrounding the city in the winter, you see a lot of people sweeping up sand after sandstorms. And the next day there'd be a sandstorm and people go out and sweep some more," Adam Smith said. "You get the sense the government, because they've moved these people, they have to create some jobs for them. But a lot of people are just given these meaningless jobs that don't have much of a point."

Ordos is one of many such examples that can be found throughout China. Of course, the ghost cities aren't designed to stay empty for long. In addition to creating jobs, the Chinese government has a plan to relocate 250 million people into cities over the coming fifteen to twenty years.

This relocation is intended to develop a more skilled working class and centralized, consumption-based economy.

By 2013, the Chinese real estate sector made up 10 percent of the entire Chinese economy, nearly double the portion just five years earlier. Land prices in China had risen 500 percent from 2000 to 2013, and shadow banking accounted for half of all borrowing in China.

In response to the pop-up shadow banking, the central government shifted its strategy. This time, rather than limit bank lending, a decision was made to limit local governments' ability to borrow from any source. However, much like Japan's window guidance quotas, there was still great pressure to report high economic growth rates. The local government officials were once again forced to get creative.

A new trend emerged in which local governments would set up new entities known as local-government funding vehicles (LGFVs) from which to borrow money. These LGFVs could be controlled by local governments without having to report what they actually owned or borrowed (much like Enron, the Texas-based energy company that hid debt off balance sheet and eventually filed bankruptcy). With these new funding vehicles, local governments could continue to approve real estate development and borrow money as needed off the official record to show increasing economic activity. These local-government funding vehicles quickly became the biggest borrowers from the shadow-banking system.

China's confusing network of backdoor loans, hidden leverage, and wild speculation is known but not widely understood. One financial analyst who has made a name for herself by understanding the details and blowing the whistle on the Chinese bubble is Charlene Chu. Chu attended Yale University, where she earned her master's degrees in international relations and business. The New York branch of the Federal Reserve hired Chu out of college to be a specialist on the Chinese financial system. While the experience was helpful, Chu wanted to go deeper. She quit her job and moved to China in 2005. Soon afterward she hired on with Fitch, one of the big-three credit-rating agencies. It was during this time that a bank executive enlightened Chu on the inner workings of how his bank repackaged loans and sold them off to investors as wealth-management products.

"It was a perfect way both to extend credit above the government's quota as well as to hide questionable loans," Chu said.

This confusing system of hidden loans was the key behind a "pervasive understatement of credit growth and credit exposure," she wrote in a 2010 report. In it, Chu claimed that China had underestimated loan growth by more than $200 billion. The following year, China's central bank agreed to change its method of accounting for lending by publishing "total social financing" rather than simply reporting bank loans as a way to try to capture more off–balance sheet lending. While the new method was an improvement, Chu continued to warn that the numbers were bigger than reported.

Chinese excess and speculation extend beyond traditional real estate. Chinese stocks rallied roughly 150 percent from the summer of 2014 to the summer of 2015. At the peak, investors were paying an average price of $140 for every $1 of net income for small-cap companies trading on the Shenzhen stock exchange. For reference, in the United States broad stock market indices have historically traded at a price of about $16 for every $1 of earnings. The value of outstanding margin loans, which are generally made to buy stock, topped 9 percent of all tradable stock in China, the highest level ever recorded.

In June 2015, the market began to fall, plunging 50 percent from the summer peak. The government intervened, even threatening prosecution for anyone who sold stock. As stock markets slowed, the government expanded its building projects. The Chinese prime minister approved development projects totaling more than $1 trillion in 2015.

Eric Sakowski runs a website dedicated to bridges. "The amount of high bridge construction in China is just insane," Sakowski said, "China's opening, say, fifty high bridges a year, and the whole of the rest of the world combined might be opening ten."

The hope behind the bridge binge is that tolls will be collected to offset the building costs. In almost every instance up to this point, tolls have been insufficient to keep pace with the costs, resulting in mounting debt and insufficient revenues. More than eighty of the one hundred tallest bridges in the world are found in China, according to Sakowski's data. Expressways in China lost $47 billion in 2015, double the loss for 2014.

"If you don't build roads, there can't be prosperity," said Huang Sanliang, a fifty-six-year-old farmer living near one of the newly constructed bridges. "But this is an expressway, not a second or third-grade road. One of those might be better for us here."

Skyscrapers are another Chinese fetish. One hundred twenty-eight skyscrapers were completed globally in 2016; nearly three-quarters were located in China. More skyscrapers were built in the city of Shenzhen alone than in the entire United States in 2016. "This path is now a dead end," said Zhao Xiao, an economist in China. "Governments can't count on the beauty of investment covering up 100 other kinds of ugliness."

"It's scary that China seems to be continuing its debt binge to achieve its unrealistic output growth targets," says Ruchir Sharma, chief global strategist with Morgan Stanley. "To me, the China economy is like a ping-pong ball falling down a steep staircase, bouncing upward temporarily when credit stimulus is added before continuing its relentless downward path."

In 2016, the size of the shadow-banking industry topped an estimated $8 trillion. According to Charlene Chu, investment allocated to wealth-management products are roughly double that of the mortgage-backed securities market that nearly leveled the US financial system in 2008. Meanwhile, household debt has increased fourfold in China since 2006.

"I don't know whether China faces a slow burn in economic growth ahead or some kind of financial crisis," said Chu. "But you can't continue on a path of allowing new credit infusions to grow at more than twice the pace of GDP growth."

Chu also estimated nonperforming loans to be $7 trillion more than officially stated. If she is correct, that would mean that roughly one-third of all outstanding loans should be considered bad debt, a far cry from the official estimate of 5.3 percent.

The International Monetary Fund also warned in 2016 about China's ballooning debt. "Since 2008, private sector debt relative to GDP has risen by 80 percentage points to about 175 percent—such large increases have internationally been associated with sharp growth slowdowns and often financial crises. . . . All credit booms that began when the ratios were above 100 percent—as in China's case—ended badly."

Forty years ago, Shenzhen was home to rice paddies and duck farms. As of 2019, Shenzhen is more than twice the size of New York City and boasts more millionaires per capita than any other city in China. Shenzhen has become the leading manufacturing city in the world and arguably China's richest city. It's now known as China's Silicon Valley. Skyscrapers dot the skyline. Palm trees and banyan trees line the city streets. Parks and open space occupy nearly 40 percent of the city's area.

Litchi Park is one of the largest parks in Shenzhen. Referred to by many as Central Park, it's reminiscent of its New York namesake. At the southern end of the park is a large billboard that attracts visitors each day, many bringing flowers and posing for pictures. On the left side of the billboard is a picture of the Shenzhen city skyline. Above the skyline written in Chinese are the words "Uphold the party's fundamental line, we will not waver in a hundred years!" On the right-hand side of the massive billboard is an image of Deng Xiaoping, the man responsible for opening the Chinese economy, who died in 1997 at the age of ninety-two as a hero to the Chinese people.

23

WRAP UP

Happy New Year. Your share of the national debt is $35,000.

— Seymour Durst, inventor of the National Debt Clock

The Great Recession of 2008–9 impacted all countries, each of which responded differently. Collectively, more than $12 trillion of asset purchases and money printing took place between the Fed, the Bank of Japan, the Bank of England, and the European Central Bank in the eight years following the financial crisis in an effort to stimulate the economy. Globally, there were 654 interest rate cuts in the eight years following Lehman Brothers' collapse. At the time of this writing in the summer of 2019, more than $15 trillion worth of bonds have negative real yields. Global debt has grown by $77 trillion since the Great Recession (an increase of roughly 45%), and no major economy has decreased its debt-to-GDP ratio since 2007. Global debt held by governments, households, and corporations now stands at 318 percent of the entire global economy.

Concern over the growing mountain of debt also isn't a new phenomenon. There is a clock in Times Square that doesn't tell the time; instead it measures the national debt and counts upward like an odometer in a moving car. Seymour Durst, a real estate developer in Manhattan, paid

$100,000 to install the clock in 1989. At the time, the national debt was $2.7 trillion. Durst was adamant that the debt would become a problem for generations to come. As early as 1980, Durst sent Christmas cards to politicians that read "Happy New Year. Your share of the national debt is $35,000."

Seymour Durst died in 1995 with the national debt approaching $5 trillion. The clock continued to tick higher day after day, until a strange thing happened. As the dot-com bubble of the 1990s grew and economic activity exploded, the government began receiving more in tax revenue from the booming economy than it was spending. Fiscal year 1999 was the first budget surplus in decades. After hitting $5.7 trillion, the national debt began to decline. Durst's clock wasn't originally designed to run backward, and it was unplugged in September 2000.

Two years later, following the bursting of the dot-com bubble, the national debt began ticking higher again and the clock was plugged in. It hasn't run backward ever since. Today, the clock reads $22 trillion.

This isn't the first time that the United States has experienced a large national debt. Following World War II, the US national debt burden surpassed 120 percent of GDP, the highest ratio in the country's history. The debt increase was primarily a function of financing a war, and the economy eventually outgrew the debt burden. Once the war ended, soldiers returned home to rejoin the workforce, start families, build homes, and buy cars. Tax revenue increased, budget deficits fell and the debt burden shrank relative to the size of the economy. The debt ratio fell to around 33 percent over the next four decades.

Outside of the United States' World War II example, there is only one recent example of an economy successfully navigating its way out of a heavy debt burden. In Ireland, national debt hit £23 billion in 1986, more than the size of all economic output in the country that year. Through a series of economic reforms, Ireland avoided a debt crisis. Most notably, Ireland took four steps: (1) corporate tax rates were reduced to attract foreign investment, (2) government spending was cut, (3) industries such as telecom, infrastructure, and air travel were largely deregulated, and (4) state-funded education began focusing on science, engineering, and technology. In essence, Ireland followed the Hayekian model of economic policy. The result was an inflow of foreign business investment eager to take advantage of the low taxes and skilled labor.

The Irish population grew from the increase in immigration, and the economy began to expand. With the expansion, tax revenue increased and the national debt began to fall relative to the size of the economy. By 2000, Ireland had a significant surplus and national debt fell to roughly half the size of the economy.

Unfortunately, the Great Recession of 2008 hit Ireland particularly hard. Much of the foreign business it attracted with the lower corporate tax rates and lax regulation was centered in the financial industry, making Ireland something of a financial hub for the Eurozone. As a result, Ireland was forced to nationalize part of the banking system during the global recession, thus increasing the national debt dramatically. By the end of 2010, the national debt was again larger than the total size of the economy. Interest rates spiked as international lenders were unwilling to make further loans to Ireland at reasonable rates. Eventually, the country accepted an €85 billion bailout loan from the IMF and European Union.

How might the recent expansion of global debt conclude? If history is any indicator, the most likely outcome will be some combination of debt restructuring, bailouts, and debt forgiveness for many countries. As demographics shift, countries with aging populations like Japan, and certain countries in Europe may be wise to rethink their obsession with economic growth and embrace quality-of-life measurements to gauge economic health rather than continued stimulus and borrowing. Time will tell whether countries are able to reframe their domestic goals and avoid a Latin American–style debt crisis.

With each debt crisis, there is a tipping point. In Latin America, it was rising interest rates; in Japan, it was a bursting real estate bubble following a change in central bank policy; in Europe, it was a crisis of confidence in the euro. Hyman Minsky was an economist with a theory about such tipping points. Minsky taught at Brown and then at University of California, Berkeley, but spent the bulk of his career at Washington University in St. Louis. He had minor academic success with his several articles and two books, but his writings failed to gain much attention before his passing in 1996.

The bulk of Minsky's work focused on the use of debt throughout the business cycle. Minsky argued, somewhat pessimistically, that good times and higher profits ultimately fuel excessive borrowing. The longer the good times last, the greater the likelihood that debt will reach extreme levels, eventually culminating in a crisis.

Minsky's theories contradicted the ideas of some of the leading economic minds at the time, who theorized that markets were efficient and investors were rational. Increases in debt, they argued, would eventually be repaid and debt bubbles would be avoided. Minsky, on the other hand, believed that markets were unstable, irrational, and complex. His theory would find renewed interest following the 2008 financial crisis in the United States.

Hyman Minsky's theory explained in financial terms what Edward Lorenz had already discovered with his butterfly presentation; that small changes in complex systems create large and unpredictable outcomes. Few would have anticipated that Paul Volcker's rate hikes would have led to malnourishment in Bolivia, or that the International Monetary Fund's austerity plan would have laid the groundwork for the boom in cocaine production in Peru. The currency manipulation agreed upon at the Plaza Hotel in 1985 couldn't have been expected to lead to increased suicide rates in Japan a decade later, but it did.

A butterfly flapped its wings on August 15, 1971, when the Nixon shock ushered in the modern era of finance. Following the abandonment of the gold standard, central banks have been free to print and manipulate currencies and interest rates as needed. Globally, central banks have shifted their mindset from sound monetary policy to an obsession with economic growth through endless stimulus and debt. The lasting impact from the Nixon shock may yet be unrealized.

The Bank of China's governor Zhou Xiaochuan warned of excessive optimism in a speech he delivered in October 2017. "If we're too optimistic when things go smoothly, tensions build up, which could lead to a sharp correction, what we call a 'Minsky Moment'. That's what we should particularly defend against."

Politicians and central bankers have a long history of forgetting the past and mistakenly fueling booms and busts, whether it be from shortsightedness or downright manipulation. Time and time again governments have attempted to spur economic growth with varying degrees of success, but never before have all governments around the world seemingly embarked on the same path at the same time. And never before has the stimulus been so massive, the result of which is a global financial system flush with debt and unbelievably low (and even negative) interest rates.

Asset values around the world have risen as a result of the stimulus measures enacted. Quality of life has improved for millions of people. By most accounts, the initial government response to the financial crisis was warranted and benefited citizens. However, the same could also be said for Japan throughout the 1980s, as asset values soared and investors profited in response to easy money and increased debt. A case could also be made that Latin America benefited tremendously from the increased debt in the 1970s, as incomes rose and infrastructure was built. In both cases, however, in an unforeseen Minsky moment, the debt burden became unsustainable and ultimately wreaked havoc on the economy. Far too many countries have relied on debt to fuel the economic recovery since the 2008 crisis, and many will likely experience a result similar to the Latin American and Japanese economies.

Thus far, the buildup in debt hasn't been a concern for many countries or investors because interest rates around the world have remained so low, and capital continues to flow freely across borders. Asset values can remain elevated for extended periods of time. Governments can manipulate interest rates and currency values for years to come. Debt can increase even further. Roads and bridges to empty cities can continue to be built in the name of economic expansion. But at some point, a butterfly will flap its wings and the economy will change again.

By remembering the past and understanding the stories that shaped our current economy, we may be able to gain insights into the future and better answer the question: What can we do today, in light of yesterday, to prepare for tomorrow?

BIBLIOGRAPHY

Introduction

Bell, Emily. 2016. "This 75 Billion Dollar Business Was Built Selling Whiskey During Prohibition . . . Legally." *VinePair*, June 9. https://vinepair.com/wine-blog/walgreens-whiskey-prescriptions-prohibition/.

Cobb, Clifford, Ted Halstead, and Jonathan Rowe. 2019. "If the GDP Is Up, Why Is America Down?" *Atlantic*, October. https://www.theatlantic.com/past/docs/politics/ecbig/gdp.htm.

Fioramonti, Lorenzo. 2017. "GDP Growth Is the Wrong Way to Measure Global Economic and Developmental Progress." *Quartz Africa*, May 29. https://qz.com/africa/993819/gdp-growth-is-the-wrong-way-to-measure-global-economic-and-developmental-progress/.

Kuznets, Simon. 1934. *National Income, 1929–1932.* 73rd US Congress, 2d session. https://fraser.stlouisfed.org/title/971.

"GDP: One of the Great Inventions of the 20th Century." *Survey of Current Business*, January. https://fraser.stlouisfed.org/files/docs/publications/SCB/pages/2000-2004/35260_2000-2004.pdf

Lorenz, Edward N., and Paul Martin. 1995. "The Essence of Chaos." *Physics Today* 48 (2): 54.

Merton, Robert K. 1936. "The Unanticipated Consequences of Purposive Social Action." *American Sociological Review* 1 (6): 894. https://doi.org/10.2307/2084615.

Winship, Scott. 2013. "The Affluent Economy: Our Misleading Obsession with Growth Rates." *Brookings*, February 25. https://www.brookings.edu/articles/the-affluent-economy-our-misleading-obsession-with-growth-rates/.

American International Group. n.d. *American Insurance Group 10-K*. http://getfilings.com/comp/k0000005272.html.

Abrams, Burton A. 2006. "How Richard Nixon Pressured Arthur Burns: Evidence from the Nixon Tapes." *Journal of Economic Perspectives* 20 (4): 177–88. https://doi.org/10.1257/jep.20.4.177.

Amadeo, Kimberly. 2019a. "Was the Big 3 Auto Bailout Worth It?" *Balance*, May 7. https://www.thebalance.com/auto-industry-bailout-gm-ford-chrysler-3305670.

Amadeo, Kimberly. 2019b. "Which President Rang Up the Highest Budget Deficit?" *Balance*, May 9. https://www.thebalance.com/deficit-by-president-what-budget-deficits-hide-3306151.

Andrews, Edmund, and Jackie Calmes. 2008. "Fed Cuts Key Rate to a Record Low." *New York Times*, December 16. https://www.nytimes.com/2008/12/17/business/economy/17fed.html.

Andrews, Edmund, Michael de la Merced, and Mary Williams Walsh. 2008. "Fed's $85 Billion Loan Rescues Insurer." *New York Times*, September 16. https://www.nytimes.com/2008/09/17/business/17insure.html.

Appelbaum, Binyamin. 2017a. "Debt Concerns, Once a Core Republican Tenet, Take a Back Seat to Tax Cuts." *New York Times*, December 2. https://www.nytimes.com/2017/12/01/us/politics/tax-cuts-deficit-debt.html.

Appelbaum, Binyamin. 2017b. "Trump's Tax Cuts Are Likely to Increase Trade Deficit." *New York Times*, November 17. https://www.nytimes.com/2017/11/17/us/politics/tax-cuts-trade-deficit-trump.html.

Bartlett, Bruce R. 2006. *Impostor: How George W. Bush Bankrupted America and Betrayed the Reagan Legacy.* New York: Doubleday.

BBC News. 2011. "Keynes v Hayek: Two Economic Giants Go Head to Head." August 2. https://www.bbc.com/news/business-14366054.

Berlin, Leslie. 2008. "Lessons of Survival, from the Dot-Com Attic." *New York Times*, November 22. https://www.nytimes.com/2008/11/23/business/23proto.html.

Bernanke, Ben S. 2002. "Deflation: Making Sure 'It' Doesn't Happen Here." Remarks before the National Economists Club, Washington, D.C., November 21. https://www.federalreserve.gov/boarddocs/speeches/2002/20021121/.

Blinder, Alan S. 1982. "The Anatomy of Double-Digit Inflation in the 1970s." In *Inflation: Causes and Effects*, edited by Robert E. Hall, 261–82. Chicago: University of Chicago Press.

Boley, John. 2001. "World Markets: Shades of Gray." *Automotive News*, July 1. http://edit.autonews.com/article/20010701/SUB/107010732/&template=print&nocache=1.

Booth, Philip. 2006. "How 364 Economists Got It Totally Wrong." *Telegraph*, March 15. https://www.telegraph.co.uk/comment/personal-view/3623669/How-364-economists-got-it-totally-wrong.html.

Boyd, Roddy. 2011. *Fatal Risk: A Cautionary Tale of AIG's Corporate Suicide.* Hoboken, NJ: John Wiley & Sons.

CBS News. 2011. "Dot-Com Flops after Huge IPOs." June 16. https://www.cbsnews.com/pictures/dot-com-flops-after-huge-ipos/.

Chan, Sewell. 2010. "The Fed? Ron Paul's Not a Fan." *New York Times*, December 11. https://www.nytimes.com/2010/12/12/weekinreview/12chan.html.

Cohan, Peter. 2012. "Dimon Principle: Open Mouth, Insert $2 Billion Foot." *Forbes*, May 11. https://www.forbes.com/sites/petercohan/2012/05/11/dimon-principle-open-mouth-insert-2-billion-foot/#4ba311d33ded.

Cohen, Adam. 2003. *The Perfect Store: Inside eBay*. New York: Back Bay Books.

Cox, Jeff. 2016. "$12 Trillion of QE and the Lowest Rates in 5,000 Years . . . for This?" *CNBC*, June 13. https://www.cnbc.com/2016/06/13/12-trillion-of-qe-and-the-lowest-rates-in-5000-years-for-this.html.

Northup, Cynthia Clark. 2003. *The American Economy: A Historical Encyclopedia*. Santa Barbara, CA: ABC-Clio.

Dash, Eric, and Andrew Ross Sorkin. 2008. "Throwing a Lifeline to a Troubled Giant." *New York Times*, September 17. https://www.nytimes.com/2008/09/18/business/18insure.html.

Domm, Patti. 2017. "Trump Economy Reaching His 3 Percent Goal Even without Tax Reform." *CNBC*, October 27. https://www.cnbc.com/2017/10/27/trump-economy-reaching-his-3-percent-goal-even-without-tax-reform.html.

Erman, Michael. 2013. "Five Years after Lehman, Americans Still Angry at Wall Street: Reuters/Ipsos Poll." *Reuters*, September 15. https://www.reuters.com/article/us-wallstreet-crisis/five-years-after-lehman-americans-still-angry-at-wall-street-reuters-ipsos-poll-idUSBRE98E06Q20130915.

Feldstein, Martin. 2013. "An Interview with Paul Volcker." *Journal of Economic Perspectives* 27 (4): 105–20. https://doi.org/10.1257/jep.27.4.105.

Field, Abigail. 2010. "Lehman Report: Why the U.S. Balked at Bailing Out Lehman." AOL.com, March 15. https://www.aol.com/2010/03/15/why-the-u-s-balked-at-bailout-out-lehman/.

Foley, Stephen. 2010. "Friedrich Hayek: Darling of the Right Is Reborn in the USA." *Independent*, July 3. https://www.independent.co.uk/news/world/americas/friedrich-hayek-darling-of-the-right-is-reborn-in-the-usa-2017267.html.

Fox, Justin. 2014. "How Economics PhDs Took Over the Federal Reserve." *Harvard Business Review*, November 2. https://hbr.org/2014/02/how-economics-phds-took-over-the-federal-reserve.

Frank, Robert. 1999. "'Detroit of the East' Big 3 Automakers Look to Asia For Growth." *Wall Street Journal*, December 19.

Gallup.com. 2016. "Presidential Approval Ratings—Barack Obama." April 21. https://news.gallup.com/poll/116479/barack-obama-presidential-job-approval.aspx.

Gallup.com. 2019. "Congress and the Public." January 15. https://news.gallup.com/poll/1600/congress-public.aspx.

Geisst, Charles R. 2018. *Beggar Thy Neighbor: A History of Usury and Debt.* Philadelphia: University of Pennsylvania Press.

Gomstyn, Alice. 2008. "Bleeding Green: The Fall of Fuld Money, Respect and the Corner Office: What Lehman's 'Gorilla' CEO Has Lost." ABC News Business Unit, October 8.

Harmer, Jerry. 2017. "20 Years on, Scars from Asian Financial Meltdown Linger." *Associated Press*, June 29. https://apnews.com/e57892c505b34f7cb2a016db6b3bc148.

Ip, Greg. 2005. "Long Study of Great Depression Shaped Bernanke's Views." *Wall Street Journal*, December 7. https://www.wsj.com/articles/SB113392265577715881.

Johnston, Eric. 2017. "Echoes of 1980s Trade War Seen in Trump Comments on Japan." *Japan Times*, January 20. https://www.japantimes.co.jp/news/2017/01/20/national/politics-diplomacy/echoes-1980s-trade-war-seen-trump-comments-japan/.

Kessler, Glenn. 2016. "Trump's Nonsensical Claim He Can Eliminate $19 Trillion in Debt in Eight Years." *Washington Post*, April 2. https://www.washingtonpost.com/news/fact-checker/wp/2016/04/02/trumps-non-sensical-claim-he-can-eliminate-19-trillion-in-debt-in-eight-years/.

Lehrman, Lewis E. 2011. "Lewis E. Lehrman: The Nixon Shock Heard 'Round the World." *Wall Street Journal*, August 15. https://www.wsj.com/articles/SB10001424053111904007304576494073418802358.

Lenzner, Robert. 2014. "Billy Salomon Turned Salomon Bros. into a Ferocious World-Class Investment Bank." *Forbes*, December 10. https://www.forbes.com/sites/robertlenzner/2014/12/10/billy-salomon-turned-salomon-bros-into-a-ferocious-world-class-investment-bank/.

Lewis, Michael. 2014. *Liar's Poker: Rising through the Wreckage on Wall Street*. New York: W. W. Norton.

Loomis, Carol, and Christine Chen. 2000. "AOL+TWX=??? Do the Math, and You Might Wonder If This Company's Long-Term Annual Return to Investors Can Beat a Treasury Bond's." *Fortune*, February 7. http://archive.

fortune.com/magazines/fortune/fortune_archive/2000/02/07/272827/ index.htm.

Lowenstein, Roger. 2001. *When Genius Failed: The Rise and Fall of Long-Term Capital Management.* New York: Random House.

Lowenstein, Roger. 2008. "Long-Term Capital Management: It's a Short-Term Memory." *New York Times*, September 7. https://www.nytimes. com/2008/09/07/business/worldbusiness/07iht-07ltcm.15941880.html.

Margaret Thatcher Foundation. 2019. "Thatcher, Hayek & Friedman." https://www.margaretthatcher.org/archive/Hayek.asp

Matthews, Chris. 2016. "Corporate America Is Drowning in Debt." *Fortune*, May 20. http://fortune.com/2016/05/20/corporate-america-debt/.

Mcgee, Suzanne. 2011. *Chasing Goldman Sachs: How the Masters of the Universe Melted Wall Street Down . . . and Why They'll Take Us to the Brink Again.* New York: Crown.

Millward, David. 2001. "Thai Financier Clears His Name." *Telegraph*, July 28. https://www.telegraph.co.uk/news/uknews/1335561/Thai-financier-clears-his-name.html.

Momani, Bessma. 2008. "Gulf Cooperation Council Oil Exporters and the Future of the Dollar." *New Political Economy* 13 (3): 293–314. https://doi. org/10.1080/13563460802302594.

Morgenson, Gretchen, and Michael Weinsten. 1998. "When Theory Met Reality: A Special Report; Teachings of Two Nobelists Also Proved Their Undoing." *New York Times*, November 14. https://www.nytimes. com/1998/11/14/business/when-theory-met-reality-special-report-teachings-two-nobelists-also-proved-their.html.

New York Times. 1974. "Simon Has Meeting with Saudi King on Investing in U.S." July 21. https://www.nytimes.com/1974/07/21/archives/simon-has-meeting-with-saudi-king-on-investing-in-us-zaki-foresees.html.

New York Times. 1982. "BUSINESS PEOPLE; A Nobel Winner Assesses Reagan." December 1. https://www.nytimes.com/1982/12/01/business/business-people-a-nobel-winner-assesses-reagan.html.

Nixon, Richard M. 2015. *Six Crises.* New York: Ishi Press International.

Ohlmacher, Scott W. 2009. "The Dissolution of the Bretton Woods System: Evidence from the Nixon Tapes August–December 1971." Undergraduate senior thesis, University of Delaware.

Quittner, Joshua, and Michelle Slatalla. 1998. *Speeding the Net: The inside Story of Netscape and How It Challenged Microsoft.* New York: Atlantic Monthly Press.

Rappeport, Alan. 2017. "Federal Debt Projected to Grow by Nearly $10 Trillion over Next Decade." *New York Times*, January 24. https://www.nytimes.com/2017/01/24/us/politics/budget-deficit-trump.html.

Reeves, Richard. 2007. *President Nixon: Alone in the White House.* New York: Simon & Schuster Paperbacks.

Reuters. 2010. "Ex-Treasury Secretaries Back Volcker Rule." *Reuters*, February 21. https://www.reuters.com/article/us-financial-regulation-secretaries/ex-treasury-secretaries-back-volcker-rule-idUSTRE61L0BB20100222.

Reuters. 2011. "Goldman Lobbying Hard to Weaken Volcker Rule." *Reuters*, May 4. https://www.reuters.com/article/goldman-volcker/goldman-lobbying-hard-to-weaken-volcker-rule-idUSN0418474320110504.

Richman, Sheldon. 2014. "The Sad Legacy of Ronald Reagan." *Freeman*, July 30. https://mises.org/library/sad-legacy-ronald-reagan-0.

Ritholtz, Barry. 2015. "The Dick Fuld Denial: Denying Responsibility Obscures the Causes of the Financial Crisis." *Bloomberg*, June 1. https://www.bloomberg.com/opinion/articles/2015-06-01/fuld-fools-himself-in-rejecting-blame-for-lehman.

Rosenbaum, David. 1989. "The Treasury's 'Mr. Diffident.'" *New York Times*, November 19. https://www.nytimes.com/1989/11/19/business/the-treasury-s-mr-diffident.html.

Schlesinger, Arthur. 2010. *A Thousand Days: John F. Kennedy in the White House*. Winnipeg: Mariner Books.

Schneiderman, R. M. 2008. "Reactions to the Fed's Rate Cut." Economix Blog. *New York Times*, December 16. https://economix.blogs.nytimes.com/2008/12/16/reactions-to-the-feds-rate-cut/.

Schulman, Bruce J. 2008. *The Seventies: The Great Shift in American Culture, Society, and Politics*. Cambridge, MA: Da Capo Press.

Severo, Richard. "John Connally of Texas, a Power in 2 Political Parties, Dies at 76." *New York Times*, June 16. www.nytimes.com/1993/06/16/us/john-connally-of-texas-a-power-in-2-political-parties-dies-at-76.html.

Shawcross, William. 1989. *The Shah's Last Ride: The Story of the Exile, Misadventures and Death of the Emperor*. London: Chatto & Windus.

GDP: One of the Great Inventions of the 20th Century." *Survey of Current Business*, January. https://fraser.stlouisfed.org/files/docs/publications/SCB/pages/2000-2004/35260_2000-2004.pdf.

Stevenson, Richard. 2000. "William E. Simon, Ex-Treasury Secretary and High-Profile Investor, Is Dead at 72." *New York Times*, June 5. https://www.nytimes.com/2000/06/05/us/william-e-simon-ex-treasury-secretary-and-high-profile-investor-is-dead-at-72.html.

Stewart, James. 2011. "Volcker Rule Grows from Simple to Complex." *New York Times*, October 21. https://www.nytimes.com/2011/10/22/business/volcker-rule-grows-from-simple-to-complex.html.

Strange, Susan, and Christopher Prout. 1976. *International Monetary Relations*. London: Oxford University Press.

Sunstein, Cass. 2017. "A Warning to Trump from Friedrich Hayek." *Bloomberg*, January 17. https://www.bloomberg.com/opinion/articles/2017-01-17/a-warning-to-trump-from-friedrich-hayek.

Taibbi, Matt. 2013. "Secrets and Lies of the Bailout." *Rolling Stone*, January 4. https://www.rollingstone.com/politics/politics-news/secrets-and-lies-of-the-bailout-113270/.

Tankersley, Jim. 2017. "Trump Makes Puzzling Claim That Rising Stock Market Erases Debt." *New York Times*, October 12. https://www.nytimes.com/2017/10/12/us/politics/trump-stock-market-national-debt-fact-check.html.

Time. 2018. "25 People to Blame for the Financial Crisis." http://content.time.com/time/specials/packages/completelist/0,29569,1877351,00.html.

Tobias, Andrew. 1982. "A Talk with Paul Volcker." *New York Times*, September 19. https://www.nytimes.com/1982/09/19/magazine/a-talk-with-paul-volcker.html.

Truong, Alice. 2015. "Netscape Changed the Internet—and the World—When It Went Public 20 Years Ago." *Quartz*, August 9. https://

qz.com/475279/netscape-changed-the-internet-and-the-world-when-it-went-public-20-years-ago-today/.

Vasel, Kathryn. 2017. "Household Debt Is Dangerously Close to 2008 Levels." *CNNMoney*, February 16. https://money.cnn.com/2017/02/16/pf/americans-more-debt-in-2016/index.html.

Volcker, Paul. 2010. "How to Reform Our Financial System." *New York Times*, January 30. https://www.nytimes.com/2010/01/31/opinion/31volcker.html.

Wapshott, Nicholas. 2012. *Keynes Hayek: The Clash That Defined Modern Economics*. New York: W. W. Norton.

Weldin, Sandra J. 2000. "A. P. Giannini, Marriner Stoddard Eccles, and the Changing Landscape of American Banking Approved." PhD dissertation, University of North Texas. https://digital.library.unt.edu/ark:/67531/metadc2489/m2/1/high_res_d/Dissertation.pdf.

Wells, Wyatt C. 1995. *Economist in an Uncertain World: Arthur F. Burns and the Federal Reserve, 1970-78*. New York: Columbia University Press.

Wicker, Tom. 1985. "In the Nation; a Deliberate Deficit." *New York Times*, July 19. https://www.nytimes.com/1985/07/19/opinion/in-the-nation-a-deliberate-deficit.html.

Williams, Mark. 2010. *Uncontrolled Risk: Lessons of Lehman Brothers and How Systemic: Lessons of Lehman Brothers and How Systemic Risk Can Still Bring down the World Financial System*. New York: McGraw-Hill Professional.

Wong, Andrea. 2016. "The Untold Story behind Saudi Arabia's 41-Year U.S. Debt Secret." *Bloomberg*, May 30. https://www.bloomberg.com/news/features/2016-05-30/the-untold-story-behind-saudi-arabia-s-41-year-u-s-debt-secret.

Latin America

AmericanForeignRelations.com. 2019. "American-Led Globalization: 1990–2001—Globalization." https://www.americanforeignrelations. com/E-N/Globalization-American-led-globalization-1990-2001.html.

Barmash, Isadore. 1991. "Wal-Mart in Venture with Mexican Store." *New York Times*, July 11. https://www.nytimes.com/1991/07/11/business/wal-mart-in-venture-with-mexican-store.html.

Beattie, Alan. 2009. *False Economy: A Surprising Economic History of the World*. New York: Riverhead Books.

Bennett, Robert. 1983a. "Citicorp Strategy in Buying Thrift Units." *New York Times*, December 17. https://www.nytimes.com/1983/12/17/business/citicorp-strategy-in-buying-thrift-units.html.

Bennett, Robert. 1983b. "Inside Citicorp." *New York Times*, May 29. https://www.nytimes.com/1983/05/29/magazine/inside-citicorp.html.

Bennett, Robert. 1984a. "Banks Plan Concession to Mexico." *New York Times*, June 6. https://www.nytimes.com/1984/06/06/business/banks-plan-concession-to-mexico.html.

Bennett, Robert. 1984b. "Mexico Aid Said to Get Backing." *New York Times*, June 5. https://www.nytimes.com/1984/06/05/business/mexico-aid-said-to-get-backing.html.

Berg, Eric. 1987a. "Bankers Pragmatic on Brazil Debt Halt." *New York Times*, February 21. https://www.nytimes.com/1987/02/21/business/bankers-pragmatic-on-brazil-debt-halt.html.

Berg, Eric. 1987b. "Brazil's Action Sends Bank Stocks Tumbling." *New York Times*, February 24. https://www.nytimes.com/1987/02/24/business/brazil-s-action-sends-bank-stocks-tumbling.html.

Berg, Eric. 1987c. "Citicorp Accepts a Big Loss Linked to Foreign Loans." *New York Times*, May 20. https://www.nytimes.com/1987/05/20/business/citicorp-accepts-a-big-loss-linked-to-foreign-loans.html.

Bloomberg News. 1997. "Wal-Mart Investing in Mexican Partner." *New York Times*, June 4. https://www.nytimes.com/1997/06/04/business/wal-mart-investing-in-mexican-partner.html.

Brooke, James. 1989. "Peru Builds Base to Combat Coca Production." *New York Times*, June 13. https://www.nytimes.com/1989/06/13/world/peru-builds-base-to-combat-coca-production.html.

Burns, Arthur. 1977. "The Need for Order in International Finance." Address to Columbia Graduate School of Business, Columbia University, New York, April 12.

Castaneda, Jorge. 1986a. "Enough Mexico-Bashing." *New York Times*, May 21. https://www.nytimes.com/1986/05/21/opinion/enough-mexico-bashing.html.

Castaneda, Jorge. 1986b. "Indebted Mexico Staggers On." *New York Times*, January 8. https://www.nytimes.com/1986/01/08/opinion/indebted-mexico-staggers-on.html.

Castaneda, Jorge. 1988. "Mexico, after Reagan and de La Madrid." *New York Times*, February 13. https://www.nytimes.com/1988/02/13/opinion/mexico-after-reagan-and-de-la-madrid.html.

Cline, William R. 1995. *International Debt Reexamined*. Washington, D.C.: Institute For International Economics.

Cottingham, Jan. 2012. "Wealth Created by Wal-Mart Supports Massive Philanthropic Efforts in Arkansas." *Arkansas Business*. July 2. https://www.arkansasbusiness.com/article/85497/wealth-created-by-wal-mart-supports-massive-philanthropic-efforts-in-arkansas.

Depalma, Anthony. 1994. "A Year to Forget: 1994 Leaves Mexico Reeling." *New York Times*, December 29. https://www.nytimes.com/1994/12/29/world/a-year-to-forget-1994-leaves-mexico-reeling.html.

Farnsworth, Clyde. 1982. "I.M.F. Loan to Mexico." *New York Times*, December 24. https://www.nytimes.com/1982/12/24/business/imf-loan-to-mexico.html.

Farnsworth, Clyde. 1984. "A Turbulent Rescue Role for the I.M.F." *New York Times*, May 4. https://www.nytimes.com/1984/05/04/business/a-turbulent-rescue-role-for-the-imf.html.

Frontline. 2014. "Interviews—Dr. Rudi Dornbusch." https://www.pbs.org/wgbh/pages/frontline/shows/mexico/interviews/dornbusch.html.

Gerth, Jeff. 1986. "International Report; Mexico's Loss of Assets Imperial's Debt Plan." *New York Times*, June 9. https://www.nytimes.com/1986/06/09/business/international-report-mexico-s-loss-assets-imperils-debt-plan-its-government-buys.html.

Gilbert, Martin. 1992. *Churchill: A Life*. New York: Holt.

Grayson, George W. 1990. *Prospects for Democracy in Mexico*. Brunswick, NJ: Transaction.

Greider, William. 1987. *Secrets of the Temple: How the Federal Reserve Runs the Country*. New York: Simon and Schuster.

Hershey, Robert. 1987. "Volcker Out after 8 Years as Federal Reserve Chief." *New York Times*, June 3. https://www.nytimes.com/1987/06/03/business/volcker-out-after-8-years-as-federal-reserve-chief-reagan-chooses-greenspan.html.

Higgins, Sean. 2015. "Clinton's Walmart Connection Fueling Left's Doubts." *Washington Examiner*, January 17. https://www.washingtonexaminer.com/clintons-walmart-connection-fueling-lefts-doubts.

Hutchinson, Kelsey. 2009. "War on Coca in Peru: An Examination of the 1980s and 1990s U.S. 'Supply Side' Policies." Seminar paper presented to the Department of History, Western Oregon University. http://www.wou.edu/history/files/2015/08/Kelsey-Hutchinson-HST-499.pdf.

Inciardi, James A., and Hilary L. Surratt. 1998. "Children in the Streets of Brazil: Drug Use, Crime, Violence, and HIV Risks." *Substance Use & Misuse* 33 (7): 1461–80. https://doi.org/10.3109/10826089809069809.

Juhasz, Antonia. 2005. "What Wal-Mart Wants from the WTO." AntoniaJuhasz.net, December 13. http://antoniajuhasz.net/article/what-wal-mart-wants-from-the-wto/.

Kilborn, Peter. 1986. "Debt Accord with Mexico Forming." *New York Times*, July 16. https://www.nytimes.com/1986/07/16/business/debt-accord-with-mexico-forming.html.

Kilborn, Peter. 1989. "U.S. Is Moving to End Doubts on Debt Proposal." *New York Times*, March 31. https://www.nytimes.com/1989/03/31/business/us-is-moving-to-end-doubts-on-debt-proposal.html.

Lev, Michael. 1997. "Thailand Shocked as Boom Goes Bust: Asian `Tiger' Economy Sinks under Weight of Its Own Successes." *Chicago Tribune*, August 31. https://www.chicagotribune.com/news/ct-xpm-1997-08-31-9709010001-story.html.

Lewis, Peter. 1994. "Attention Shoppers: Internet Is Open." *New York Times*, August 12. https://www.nytimes.com/1994/08/12/business/attention-shoppers-internet-is-open.html.

Matt, Moffett. 1991. "Mexican Retailers Jockey for Position, Hoping to Win Big as Nation Recovers." *Wall Street Journal,* August 26.

Moreton, Bethany. 2010. *To Serve God and Wal-Mart: The Making of Christian Free Enterprise.* Cambridge, MA: Harvard University Press.

Nash, Nathaniel. 1986. "Investing; Mexican Jitters Discounted." *New York Times,* June 15. https://www.nytimes.com/1986/06/15/business/investing-mexican-jitters-discounted.html.

New York Times. 1982. "Brazil's Debt and Promise," December 2. https://www.nytimes.com/1982/12/02/opinion/brazil-s-debt-and-promise.html

New York Times. 1985. "Support Urged for Debt Plan," December 3. https://www.nytimes.com/1985/12/03/business/support-urged-for-debt-plan.html

New York Times. 1988. "Brazil Plans Talks on Debt," May 5. https://www.nytimes.com/1988/05/05/business/brazil-plans-talks-on-debt.html

New York Times. 1989. "Relief for Foreign Debtors, at Last," March 14. https://www.nytimes.com/1989/03/14/opinion/relief-for-foreign-debtors-at-last.html

Passell, Peter. 1989a. "Economic Scene; Shuffling toward Debt Reduction." *New York Times,* March 22. https://www.nytimes.com/1989/03/22/business/economic-scene-shuffling-toward-debt-reduction.html.

Passell, Peter. 1989b. "Economic Scene; Shuffling toward Debt Reduction." *New York Times,* March 22. https://www.nytimes.com/1989/03/22/business/economic-scene-shuffling-toward-debt-reduction.html.

Paxson, Christina, and Nobert Schady. 2005. "Child Health and Economic Crisis in Peru." *World Bank Economic Review* 19 (2): 203–23. https://doi.org/10.1093/wber/lhi011.

Pine, Art. 1989. "Baker Admits Latin Debt Plan Failed, Urges New Strategy." *Los Angeles Times*, January 18. http://articles.latimes.com/1989-01-18/business/fi-651_1_debt-strategy.

Quint, Michael. 1988. "The Financier 'Who Knows What Is Going On.'" *New York Times*, August 6. https://www.nytimes.com/1988/08/06/us/the-financier-who-knows-what-is-going-on.html.

Quint, Michael. 1989a. "Bankers Cool to Appeal by Brady on Debt Plan." *New York Times*, June 6. https://www.nytimes.com/1989/06/06/business/bankers-cool-to-appeal-by-brady-on-debt-plan.html.

Quint, Michael. 1989b. "Mexico Aid Package Spurs Talk with Banks." *New York Times*, June 8.

Rabinovich, Abraham. 2017. *The Yom Kippur War: The Epic Encounter That Transformed the Middle East.* New York: Schocken Books.

Richman, Louis, and David Kirkpatrick. 2019. "Who Is Nick Brady? Why It Matters. *Fortune*, May 22. http://archive.fortune.com/magazines/fortune/fortune_archive/1989/05/22/72007/index.htm.

Riding, Alan. 1982a. "Man in the News; Survivor: Jesus Silva Herzog." *New York Times*, August 21. https://www.nytimes.com/1982/08/21/business/man-in-the-news-survivor-jesus-silva-herzog.html.

Riding, Alan. 1982b. "Mexico Agrees to Austerity Terms for $3.84 Billion in I.M.F. Credit." *New York Times*, November 11. https://www.nytimes.com/1982/11/11/business/mexico-agrees-to-austerity-terms-for-3.84-billion-in-imf-credit.html.

Riding, Alan. 1982c. "Mexico's President-Elect to Meet with Reagan in San Diego Today." *New York Times*, October 8. https://www.nytimes.com/1982/10/08/world/mexico-s-president-elect-to-meet-with-reagan-in-san-diego-today.html.

Riding, Alan. 1984a. "Brazil's Plan for Rescheduling Debt." *New York Times*, November 12. https://www.nytimes.com/1984/11/12/business/brazil-s-plan-for-rescheduling-debt.html.

Riding, Alan. 1984b. "Citibank Flourishes in Brazil." *New York Times*, December 3. https://www.nytimes.com/1984/12/03/business/citibank-florishes-in-brazil.html.

Riding, Alan. 1985a. "Brazil to Try to Revamp Debt before I.M.F. Pact." *New York Times*, November 27. https://www.nytimes.com/1985/11/27/business/brazil-to-try-to-revamp-debt-before-imf-pact.html.

Riding, Alan. 1985b. "International Report; Anxiety Growing over Peru's Debt." *New York Times*, April 22.

Riding, Alan. 1986. "Peru Faces Credit Bar by the I.M.F." *New York Times*, August 15. https://www.nytimes.com/1986/08/15/business/peru-faces-credit-bar-by-the-imf.html.

Riding, Alan. 1987a. "Brazilian Debt Crisis Flares Again." *New York Times*, February 16. https://www.nytimes.com/1987/02/16/business/brazilian-debt-crisis-flares-again.html.

Riding, Alan. 1987b. "Brazil's Crippling Inflation." *New York Times*, May 30. https://www.nytimes.com/1987/05/30/business/brazil-s-crippling-inflation.html.

Riding, Alan. 1987c. "Brazil to Suspend Interest Payment to Foreign Banks." *New York Times*, February 21. https://www.nytimes.com/1987/02/21/business/brazil-to-suspend-interest-payment-to-foreign-banks.html.

Riding, Alan. 1988a. "As Peru's Crisis Grows, Drastic Steps Are Urged." *New York Times*, November 30. https://www.nytimes.com/1988/11/30/world/as-peru-s-crisis-grows-drastic-steps-are-urged.html.

Riding, Alan. 1988b. "International Report; Brazil's Reversal of Debt Strategy." *New York Times*, February 22. https://www.nytimes.com/1988/02/22/business/international-report-brazil-s-reversal-of-debt-strategy.html.

Riding, Alan. 1988c. "Peru, in Disarray, Directs Its Fury at the President." *New York Times*, October 19. https://www.nytimes.com/1988/10/19/world/peru-in-disarray-directs-its-fury-at-the-president.html.

Roddick, Jacqueline. 1988. *The Dance of the Millions: Latin America and the Debt Crisis.* London: Latin America Bureau.

Rohter, Larry. 1986. "Mexico's New Type of Emigrant: Well-to-Do, Skilled, Disillusioned." *New York Times*, October 21. https://www.nytimes.com/1986/10/21/world/mexico-s-new-type-of-emigrant-well-to-do-skilled-disillusioned.html.

Rohter, Larry. 1987a. "Mexico Battles Drugs Anew; Says War Is Far from Over." *New York Times*, June 15. https://www.nytimes.com/1987/06/15/world/mexico-battles-drugs-anew-says-war-is-far-from-over.html.

Rohter, Larry. 1987b. "Mexico City Journal; as Land Sinks into Debt, Can Poor Stay Afloat?" *New York Times*, June 9. https://www.nytimes.com/1987/06/09/world/mexico-city-journal-as-land-sinks-into-debt-can-poor-stay-afloat.html.

Rohter, Larry. 1988. "Mexicans Say They Can't Lose No Matter Who Wins the White House." *New York Times*, September 13. https://www.nytimes.com/1988/09/13/us/mexicans-say-they-can-t-lose-no-matter-who-wins-the-white-house.html.

Romano, Lois. 1989. "The Casual Force of Nick Brady." *Washington Post*, April 25. https://www.washingtonpost.com/archive/lifestyle/1989/04/25/the-casual-force-of-nick-brady/706d7660-79cb-49c7-8bb1-7dcd85352f0d/.

Rowe, James. 1986. "Mexico Again on the Brink in Debt Crisis." *Washington Post*, June 8. https://www.washingtonpost.com/archive/business/1986/06/08/mexico-again-on-the-brink-in-debt-crisis/14603c8c-d094-46ec-8260-9552d5302e81/.

Sachs, Jeffrey. 1987. "Business Forum: Should Some Latin Debt Be Forgiven? It's the Right Time to Offer Real Relief." *New York Times*, August 9. https://www.nytimes.com/1987/08/09/business/business-forum-should-some-latin-debt-be-forgiven-it-s-right-time-offer-real.html.

Sachs, Jeffrey, Aaron Tornell, and Andres Velasco. 1995. "The Collapse of the Mexican Peso: What Have We Learned?" NBER Working Paper No. 5142, National Bureau of Economic Research, June. https://www.nber.org/papers/w5142.

Sanger, David, and Anthony Depalma. 1995. "U.S. Bailout of Mexico Verging on Success or Dramatic Failure." *New York Times*, April 2. https://www.nytimes.com/1995/04/02/business/us-bailout-of-mexico-verging-on-success-or-dramatic-failure.html.

Shenon, Philip. 1988. "Meese Sees Peru Drug Fields and Promises Better Action." *New York Times*, April 11. https://www.nytimes.com/1988/04/11/world/meese-sees-peru-drug-fields-and-promises-better-action.html.

Silk, Leonard. 1982. "Economic Scene; Less Jittery Financiers." *New York Times*, September 15. https://www.nytimes.com/1982/09/15/business/economic-scene-less-jittery-financiers.html.

Silk, Leonard. 1985. "Economic Scene; Still a Lot to Do on World Debt." *New York Times*, February 15. https://www.nytimes.com/1985/02/15/business/economic-scene-still-a-lot-to-do-on-world-debt.html.

Silk, Leonard. 1989. "Economic Scene; Third World Debt: The Brady Plan." *New York Times*, March 31. https://www.nytimes.com/1989/03/31/business/economic-scene-third-world-debt-the-brady-plan.html.

Sims, Jocelyn, and Jessie Romero. 2013. "Latin American Debt Crisis of the 1980s: Federal Reserve History." FederalReserveHistory.org. https://www.federalreservehistory.org/essays/latin_american_debt_crisis.

Stockton, William. 1985. "I.M.F. and Mexico in Post-Quake Talk." *New York Times*, October 31. https://www.nytimes.com/1985/10/31/business/imf-and-mexico-in-post-quake-talk.html.

Stockton, William. 1986. "Mexico City Journal; Seeking the Killer Quake's Architects." *New York Times*, November 29. https://www.nytimes.com/1986/11/29/world/mexico-city-journal-seeking-the-killer-quake-s-architects.html.

Wayne, Leslie. 1984. "Citi's Soaring Ambition." *New York Times*, June 24. https://www.nytimes.com/1984/06/24/business/citi-s-soaring-ambition.html.

Weisman, Peter. 1989. "Japan Takes a Leading Role in the Third-World Debt Crisis." *New York Times*, April 17. https://www.nytimes.com/1989/04/17/business/japan-takes-a-leading-role-in-the-third-world-debt-crisis.html.

White House. 2019. "The Clinton Presidency: A Foreign Policy for the Global Age." https://clintonwhitehouse5.archives.gov/WH/Accomplishments/eightyears-10.html.

World Bank Group Archives, Folder Title: Briefing Papers: Visit to Mexico, March 2-6, 1982 - Briefings 01, Folder ID: 1774021, Dates: 3/1/1982 - 3/31/1982, World Bank Group Archives, Washington, D.C., United States.

Yergin, Daniel. 2012. *The Prize: The Epic Quest for Oil, Money & Power*. London: Simon & Schuster.

Zweig, Phillip L. 1995. *Wriston: Walter Wriston, Citibank and the Rise and Fall of American Financial Supremacy*. New York: Crown Publishers.

Japan
Adelson, Andrea. 1987. "Business People; Japan's Bidder for Dunes Has International Goal." *New York Times*, August 10. https://www.nytimes.com/1987/08/10/business/business-people-japan-s-bidder-for-dunes-has-international-goal.html.

Applegate, Jane. 1990. "Japanese Developer to Buy All of Pebble Beach Co." *Los Angeles Times*. September 6. https://www.latimes.com/archives/la-xpm-1990-09-06-fi-946-story.html.

Ashburn, A. 1977. Toyota's "Famous Ohno System." *American Machinist*, July.

Associated Press. 1986. "Japanese Bank Is Largest." *New York Times*, July 31.

Bates, James. 1992. "Japan's U.S. Real Estate Buying Plunges." *Los Angeles Times*. February 21. https://www.latimes.com/archives/la-xpm-1992-02-21-mn-2588-story.html.

Below, Bill. 2016. "The Case of the Shrinking Country: Japan's Demographic and Policy Challenges in 5 Charts." *OECD Insights Blog*.

April 11. http://oecdinsights.org/2016/04/11/the-case-of-the-shrinking-country-japans-demographic-and-policy-challenges-in-5-charts/.

Bloomberg News. 1997. "Ex-Head of Tainted Japan Bank, under Inquiry, Commits Suicide." *New York Times*, June 30. https://www.nytimes.com/1997/06/30/business/ex-head-of-tainted-japan-bank-under-inquiry-commits-suicide.html.

Bloomberg News. 1998. "Acting Quickly, Japan Seizes a 2d Big and Failing Bank." *New York Times*, December 14. https://www.nytimes.com/1998/12/14/business/acting-quickly-japan-seizes-a-2d-big-and-failing-bank.html.

Brooke, James. 2002. "They're Alive! They're Alive! Not! Japan Hesitates to Put an End to Its 'Zombie' Businesses." *New York Times*, October 29. https://www.nytimes.com/2002/10/29/business/they-re-alive-they-re-alive-not-japan-hesitates-put-end-its-zombie-businesses.html.

Button, Adam. 2016. "BOJ Is a Top-10 Shareholder of 90% of Japan's Stock Market." *ForexLive*, April 24. https://www.nasdaq.com/article/boj-is-a-top-10-shareholder-of-90-of-japans-stock-market-cm610733.

Chen, Hongyi, Michael Funke, and Ivan Lozev. 2017. "To Guide or Not to Guide? Quantitative Monetary Policy Tools and Macroeconomic Dynamics in China." *SSRN Electronic Journal*. https://doi.org/10.2139/ssrn.2980537.

Chicago Tribune. 1991. "Pebble Beach Owner Apologizes." December 30. https://www.chicagotribune.com/news/ct-xpm-1991-12-30-9104270064-story.html.

Chira, Susan. 1986. "International Report; the Japanese Bank That Is Now No.1." *New York Times*, September 8. https://www.nytimes.com/1986/09/08/business/international-report-the-japanese-bank-that-is-now-no-1.html.

Cusumano, Michael A. 1988. "Manufacturing Innovation: Lessons from the Japanese Auto Industry." *MIT Sloan Management Review.* October 15. https://sloanreview.mit.edu/article/manufacturing-innovation-lessons-from-the-japanese-auto-industry/.

De, Andrea, Andrea De Michelis, and Matteo Iacoviello. 2016. "Raising an Inflation Target: The Japanese Experience with Abenomics." *European Economic Review* 88 (C): 67–87. https://econpapers.repec.org/article/eeeeecrev/v_3a88_3ay_3a2016_3ai_3ac_3ap_3a67-87.htm.

Dowie, Mark. 1977. "Pinto Madness." *Mother Jones*, September. https://www.motherjones.com/politics/1977/09/pinto-madness/.

Economist. "Land of the Setting Sun." 2009. November 12. https://www.economist.com/business/2009/11/12/land-of-the-setting-sun

Fackler, Martin. 2013. "Hope in Japan That Shinzo Abe's 'Abenomics' May Be a Cure." *New York Times*, May 20. https://www.nytimes.com/2013/05/21/world/asia/hope-in-japan-that-abenomics-may-be-turning-things-around.html.

Fallows, James. 1989. "Containing Japan." *Atlantic*, May. https://www.theatlantic.com/magazine/archive/1989/05/containing-japan/376337/.

Fukumoto, Tomoyuki, Masato Higashi, Yasunari Inamura, and Takeshi Kimura. 2010. "Effectiveness of Window Guidance and Financial Environment In Light of Japan's Experience of Financial Liberalization and a Bubble Economy." *Bank of Japan Review* 2010-E-4 (August): 1–11. https://www.boj.or.jp/en/research/wps_rev/rev_2010/data/rev10e04.pdf.

Greenberg, Larry. 2010. "Looking Back at the Plaza and Louvre Currency Accords—Currency Thoughts." CurrencyThoughts.com, October 21. http://currencythoughts.com/2010/10/21/looking-back-at-the-plaza-and-louvre-currency-accords/.

Haire, Meaghan. 2009. "The Walkman." *Time*, July 1. http://content.time.com/time/nation/article/0,8599,1907884,00.html.

Harrington, Patrick. 2017. "Hiking in a Forest Born out of Mount Fuji's Lava." *New York Times*, January 18. https://www.nytimes.com/2017/01/18/travel/hiking-aokigahara-forest-japan-mount-fuji-lava.html?mcubz=1&_r=0.

Holusha, John. 1983. "'Just-in-Time' System Cuts Japan's Auto Costs." *New York Times*, March 25. https://www.nytimes.com/1983/03/25/business/just-in-time-system-cuts-japan-s-auto-costs.html.

Hylton, Richard, and Joyce Davis. 1995. "Behind the Fall of the Rockefeller Center; the Inside Story of Why Bad Blood Separates the Rockefellers and Mitsubishi—and Taints the Next Round of Bitter Fighting." CNN.com, July 10. https://money.cnn.com/magazines/fortune/fortune_archive/1995/07/10/204272/index.htm.

Ito, Takatoshi. n.d. "Japanese Monetary Policy: 1998-2005 and Beyond." Accessed May 24, 2019. https://www.bis.org/publ/bppdf/bispap31i.pdf.

Japan Property Central. 2016. "Japan's New Apartment Price-to-Income Ratios Reach 24 Year High." August 5. http://japanpropertycentral.com/2016/08/japans-new-apartment-price-to-income-ratios-reach-24-year-high/.

Joffe-Walt, Chana. 2010. "The Secret Plan to Fix the Dollar." National Public Radio, December 17. https://www.npr.org/sections/money/2010/12/17/132142673/plaza-accord.

Jordan, Mary, and Kevin Sullivan. 1998. "Bank Inspectors Held in Tokyo Crackdown." *Washington Post*, January 27.

Joseph, Damian. 2009. "Ugliest Cars of the Past 50 Years." *Bloomberg Businessweek*, October 30.

Kihara, Leika. 2016. "BOJ Eases Policy by Doubling ETF Buying, Underwhelms Expectations." *Reuters*, July 29. https://www.reuters.com/article/us-japan-economy-boj/boj-eases-policy-by-doubling-etf-buying-underwhelms-expectations-idUSKCN1090AY.

Leggett, Christopher. 2019. "The Ford Pinto Case." https://users.wfu.edu/palmitar/Law&Valuation/Papers/1999/Leggett-pinto.html.

Los Angeles Times. "Rockefeller Center Deal by Japanese Firm Draws Mixed Reaction in N.Y." 1989. LATimes.com, November 1. https://www.latimes.com/archives/la-xpm-1989-11-01-fi-205-story.html

Lienert, Dan. 2004. "The Worst Cars of All Time." *Forbes*, January 27.

Lipscy, Phillip, and Hirofumi Takinami. 2013. "The Politics of Financial Crisis Response in Japan and the United States." *Japanese Journal of Political Science* 14 (3): 321–53, https://doi.org/10.1017/s1468109913000133.

Lohr, Steve. 2011. "Maybe Japan Was Just a Warm-Up to the Rivalry with China." *New York Times*, January 22. https://www.nytimes.com/2011/01/23/business/23japan.html.

Neil, Dan. 2007. "1971 Ford Pinto—the 50 Worst Cars of All Time." *Time*, September 7.

New York Times. 1988. "Greenspan Sees Harm If Dollar Falls Further." June 9. https://www.nytimes.com/1988/06/09/business/greenspan-sees-harm-if-dollar-falls-further.html

Newsweek. 1991. "What Japan Will Buy Next." November 10. https://www.newsweek.com/what-japan-will-buy-next-201756.

Noguchi, Yukio, and James Poterba. 1994. *Housing Markets in the U.S. and Japan*. Chicago: University of Chicago Press. https://www.nber.org/chapters/c8818.pdf.

Pinder, Jeanne. 1993. "Headache for Japanese Investors." *New York Times*, June 2. https://www.nytimes.com/1993/06/02/business/headache-for-japanese-investors.html.

Pollack, Andrew. 1994. "Japan to End Restraints on Auto Exports to U.S." *New York Times*, March 29. https://www.nytimes.com/1994/03/29/business/japan-to-end-restraints-on-auto-exports-to-us.html.

Powell, Bill. 2009. "Japan, after the Bubble." *Time*, June 18. http://content.time.com/time/specials/packages/article/0,28804,1902809_1902810_1905192,00.html.

Rhodes, James, and Naoyuki Yoshino. 2004. "Japan's Monetary Policy Transition, 1955–2004." http://fmwww.bc.edu/repec/esFEAM04/up.30042.1080738722.pdf.

Roman, Hobart. 1993. "Japan's Secret: W. Edward Deming," *Washington Post*, December 23.

Roth, Martin. 1989. *Making Money in Japanese Stocks*. Rutland, VT: Charles E. Tuttle.

Sterngold, James. 1995. "Japanese Are in Rush to Sell Their Real Estate in the U.S." *New York Times*, June 9. https://www.nytimes.com/1995/06/09/business/japanese-are-in-rush-to-sell-their-real-estate-in-the-us.html.

Strom, Stephanie. 2000. "International Business; in Japan Banker's Suicide, Hints of Debt Burden's Human Toll." *New York Times*, September 22. https://www.nytimes.com/2000/09/22/business/international-business-japan-banker-s-suicide-hints-debt-burden-s-human-toll.html.

Sugawara, S. 1998. "Bank Official Found Dead in Japan." *Washington Post*, May 3.

Takeo, Yuko, Min Jeong Lee, and Toshiro Hasegawa. 2017. "Japan's Central Bank Is Distorting the Market, Bourse Chief Says." *Bloomberg*, July 19. https://www.bloomberg.com/news/articles/2017-07-19/japan-bourse-head-turns-surprise-critic-of-kuroda-etf-purchases.

Tierney, John. 1994. "Porn, the Low-Slung Engine of Progress." *New York Times*, January 9. https://www.nytimes.com/1994/01/09/arts/porn-the-low-slung-engine-of-progress.html.

Tong, Carl H., and Allen L. Bures. 2019. "The Voluntary Export Restraint (VER) Agreement with Japan on Automobiles in the 1980s." *Essays in Economic & Business History* 21 (0). http://www.ebhsoc.org/journal/index.php/journal/article/view/97.

Vogel, Ezra F. 1979. *Japan as Number One Lessons for America*. Cambridge, MA: Harvard University Press.

Vogel, Ezra F. 2001. *Japan as Number One: Lessons for America*. Lincoln, NE: iUniverse.Com.

Wudunn, Sheryl. 1997. "Japan to Rescue 2 Top-Tier Banks from Bad Debt." *New York Times*, April 2. https://www.nytimes.com/1997/04/02/business/japan-to-rescue-2-top-tier-banks-from-bad-debt.html.

Wudunn, Sheryl. 1998. "International Business; Tokyo Appears Close to Taking Over a Big Bank." *New York Times*, December 12. https://www.nytimes.com/1998/12/12/business/international-business-tokyo-appears-close-to-taking-over-a-big-bank.html.

Europe

Barber, Lionel, and Michael Steen. 2012. "FT Person of the Year: Mario Draghi." *Financial Times*, December 13. https://www.ft.com/content/8fca75b8-4535-11e2-838f-00144feabdc0.

Cheng, Evelyn. 2016. "Why Big Investors Including BlackRock Are Buying Negative-Yielding Debt." Yahoo.com, September 9. https://finance.yahoo.com/news/why-big-investors-including-blackrock-180341754.html.

Coakley, Caitlin, Daniel Reed, and Shane Taylor. 2009. "Gross Domestic Product by State Advance Statistics for 2008 and Revised Statistics for 2005–2007." https://apps.bea.gov/scb/pdf/2009/06%20June/0609_gdp_state.pdf.

Coy, Peter, and Paul Gordon. 2019. "Is the World Overdoing Low Interest Rates?" *Bloomberg*, June 6. https://www.bloomberg.com/news/articles/2017-06-06/are-low-interest-rates-bad-for-growth.

Davis, Owen. 2015. "Greek Debt Crisis: How Did Greece Get Here and Where Is It Going?" *International Business Times*, July 1. https://www.ibtimes.com/greek-debt-crisis-how-did-greece-get-here-where-it-going-1992390.

DiChristopher, Tom. 2016. "Live Blog Recap: Buffett on Stocks, Economy & More." CNBC, February 29. https://www.cnbc.com/2016/02/29/live-blog-3-hours-with-warren-buffett.html.

Dougherty, Carter. 2009. "Poland Gets $20 Billion Credit Line from I.M.F." *New York Times*, April 14. https://www.nytimes.com/2009/04/15/business/global/15imf.html.

Duxbury, Charles, and David Gauthier-Villars. 2016. "Negative Rates around the World: How One Danish Couple Gets Paid Interest on Their Mortgage." *Wall Street Journal*, April 14. https://www.wsj.com/articles/the-upside-down-world-of-negative-interest-rates-1460643111.

Erlanger, Steven. 2009. "Economy Shows Cracks in European Union." *New York Times*, June 8. https://www.nytimes.com/2009/06/09/world/europe/09union.html.

Ewing, Jack. 2014. "European Central Bank Chief Looks for Silver Bullet." *New York Times*, June 3. https://www.nytimes.com/2014/06/04/business/international/european-central-bank-chief-looks-for-silver-bullet.html.

Geewax, Marilyn. 2015. "The Downside of Keeping Interest Rates So Low for So Long," WBUR.org, September 16. https://www.wbur.org/npr/438968019/the-downside-of-keeping-interest-rates-so-low-for-so-long.

Gutner, Tamar. 2016. "Evaluating the IMF's Performance in the Global Financial Crisis." WRLC.org. https://auislandora.wrlc.org/islandora/object/auislandora%3A65059.

Jolly, David, and Katrin Bennhold. 2008. "European Leaders Agree to Inject Cash into Banks." *New York Times*, October 12. https://www.nytimes.com/2008/10/13/business/13europe.html.

Karnitschnig, Matthew. 2015. "Greece Struggles to Get Citizens to Pay Their Taxes." *Wall Street Journal*, February 25. https://www.wsj.com/articles/greece-struggles-to-get-citizens-to-pay-their-taxes-1424867495.

Krugman, Paul. 2011. "The Road to Economic Crisis Is Paved with Euros." *New York Times*, January 12. https://www.nytimes.com/2011/01/16/magazine/16Europe-t.html.

Krugman, Paul. 2012. "Crash of the Bumblebee." *New York Times*, July 30. https://www.nytimes.com/2012/07/30/opinion/krugman-crash-of-the-bumblebee.html.

Mody, Ashoka. 2018. *EuroTragedy: A Drama in Nine Acts*. New York: Oxford University Press.

Zeng, Min. 2015. "Government Bond Yields Turn Negative." *Wall Street Journal*, January 14. https://www.wsj.com/articles/government-bond-yields-turn-negative-1421257217.

Young, Angelo. 2015. "Why China Is Launching Massive $1.1 Trillion Stimulus Package." *International Business Times*, January 6. https://www.ibtimes.com/why-china-launching-massive-11-trillion-stimulus-package-1774610.

China

Barboza, David. 2010a. "A New Chinese City, with Everything but People." *New York Times*, October 19. https://www.nytimes.com/2010/10/20/business/global/20ghost.html.

Barboza, David. 2010b. "China's Real Estate Boom and Conflicting Policy." *New York Times*, August 1. https://www.nytimes.com/2010/08/02/business/global/02chinareal.html.

Bell, David, and Mary Shelman. 2011. "KFC's Radical Approach to China." *Harvard Business Review*. August. https://hbr.org/2011/11/kfcs-radical-approach-to-china.

Bildner, Eli. 2013. "Ordos: A Ghost Town That Isn't." *Atlantic*, April 8. https://www.theatlantic.com/china/archive/2013/04/ordos-a-ghost-town-that-isnt/274776/.

Bloomberg News. 2017. "China's $8.5 Trillion Shadow Bank Industry Is Back in Full Swing." April 18. https://www.bloomberg.com/news/articles/2017-04-18/china-s-8-5-trillion-shadow-bank-industry-is-back-in-full-swing.

Bradsher, Keith. 2009. "Some See China's Buying Spree on Commodities as Short-Lived." *New York Times*, June 10. https://www.nytimes.com/2009/06/11/business/economy/11commodity.html.

Buckley, Chris. 2017. "China's New Bridges: Rising High, but Buried in Debt." *New York Times*, June 10. https://www.nytimes.com/2017/06/10/world/asia/china-bridges-infrastructure.html.

Burns, John. 1985. "China's 'Open Door' to West Begins to Close." *New York Times*, August 4. https://www.nytimes.com/1985/08/04/world/china-s-open-door-to-west-begins-to-close.html.

Chang, Gordon G. 2015. "Did China Just Launch World's Biggest Spending Plan?" *Forbes*, May 24. https://www.forbes.com/sites/gordon-chang/2015/05/24/did-china-just-launch-worlds-biggest-spending-plan/#570de5d32f13.

DeWolf, Christopher. 2017. "Shenzhen's Never-Ending Skyscraper Boom." CNN, July 24. https://www.cnn.com/style/article/shenzhen-sky-scraper/index.html.

Elliott, Douglas, Arthur Kroeber, and Yu Qiao. 2015. "Shadow Banking in China: A Primer." *Economic Studies at Brookings*, March. https://www.brookings.edu/wp-content/uploads/2016/06/shadow_banking_china_elliott_kroeber_yu.pdf.

Evans, Peter. 2016. "Toxic Loans around the World Weigh on Global Growth." *New York Times*, February 3. https://www.nytimes.com/2016/02/04/business/dealbook/toxic-loans-in-china-weigh-on-global-growth.html.

Frangos, Alex. 2013. "Charlene Chu Is the 'Rock Star' of Chinese Debt Analysis." *Wall Street Journal*, August 23. https://www.wsj.com/articles/charlene-chu-is-the-rock-star-of-chinese-debt-analysis-1377227878.

French, Howard. 2006. "Chinese Success Story Chokes on Its Own Growth." *New York Times*, December 19. https://www.nytimes.com/2006/12/19/world/asia/19shenzhen.html.

International Institute for Sustainable Development. 2016. "Rethinking Investments in Natural Resources: China's Emerging Role in the Mekong Region (Policy Brief)." January 16. https://www.iisd.org/library/rethinking-investments-natural-resources-chinas-emerging-role-mekong-region-policy-brief

Laing, Jonathan R. 2016. "China's Debt Addiction Could Lead to a Financial Crisis." *Barrons*, November 5. https://www.barrons.com/articles/chinas-debt-addiction-could-lead-to-a-financial-crisis-1478322658.

Larry, Summers. 2016. "The Age of Secular Stagnation." *Foreign Affairs*, February 15. http://larrysummers.com/2016/02/17/the-age-of-secular-stagnation/.

O'Donnell, Mary Ann, Winnie Wong, and Jonathan Bach. 2017. *Learning from Shenzhen: China's Post-Mao Experiment from Special Zone to Model City*. Chicago: University of Chicago Press.

McMillan, Alex Frew. 2010. "New Analysis of China's Real Estate Market Shows 'Dramatic' Growth." *New York Times*, January 7. https://www.nytimes.com/2010/01/08/greathomesanddestinations/08iht-reprice.html.

Meunier, Sophie. 2019. "Beware of Chinese Bearing Gifts: Why China's Direct Investment Poses Political Challenges in Europe and the United States." Oxford: Oxford University Press. https://scholar.princeton.edu/smeunier/publications/beware-chinese-bearing-gifts-why-chinas-direct-investment-poses-political.

New York Times. 2015. "China's Unsettling Stock Market Boom." June 15. https://www.nytimes.com/2015/06/15/opinion/chinas-unsettling-stock-market-boom.htm

Rampell, Catherine. 2011. "Sure Cure for Debt Problems Is Economic Growth." *New York Times*, July 30. https://www.nytimes.com/2011/07/31/business/economy/sure-cure-for-debt-problems-is-economic-growth.html.

Reuters. 2010. "China's Bank Regulator Keeps Close Eye on Real Estate Market." *New York Times*, August 6. https://archive.nytimes.com/query.nytimes.com/gst/fullpage-9C0CE5D9123EF935A3575BC0A9669D8B63.html.

Reuters. 2012. "New Investment Products in China Raise Fears of Collapse." *New York Times*, August 6. https://www.nytimes.com/2012/08/07/business/global/new-investment-products-in-china-raise-fears-of-collapse.html.

Schuman, Michael. 2016. "China's Big Debt Worries George Soros. Should It Worry You?" *New York Times*, September 8. https://www.nytimes.com/2016/09/08/business/dealbook/chinas-big-debt-worries-george-soros-should-it-worry-you.html?mcubz=2&_r=0.

Swanson, Ana. 2015. "How China Used More Cement in 3 Years than the U.S. Did in the Entire 20th Century." *Washington Post*, March 24. https://www.washingtonpost.com/news/wonk/wp/2015/03/24/how-china-used-more-cement-in-3-years-than-the-u-s-did-in-the-entire-20th-century/.

Tu, Lianting, Narae Kim, and Carrie Hong. 2017. "Risk Comes Home as LGFV Dollar Debt Cocktails Sold in China." *Bloomberg*, February 9. https://www.bloomberg.com/news/articles/2017-02-09/dollar-bonds-of-china-s-city-builders-packaged-into-risky-punch.

Turner, Grant, Nicholas Tan, and Dena Sadeghian. 2012. "The Chinese Banking System." *Bulletin*, September. https://www.rba.gov.au/publications/bulletin/2012/sep/7.html.

Wren, Christopher. 1982a. "China's Courtship of Capitalism." *New York Times*, April 25.

Wren, Christopher. 1982b. "China Unleashes a Capitalist Tool." *New York Times*, April 25.

Debt Clock

Allen, Katie. 2017. "Quantitative Easing around the World: Lessons from Japan, UK and US." *Guardian*, July 14. https://www.theguardian.com/business/2015/jan/22/quantitative-easing-around-the-world-lessons-from-japan-uk-and-us.

Dolan, Matthew. 2009. "To Outfox the Chicken Tax, Ford Strips Its Own Vans." *Wall Street Journal*, September 23. https://www.wsj.com/articles/SB125357990638429655.

Dorney, John. 2011. "Life and Debt—a Short History of Public Spending, Borrowing and Debt in Independent Ireland." *Irish Story*, January 25. http://www.theirishstory.com/2011/01/25/life-and-debt-%E2%80%93-a-short-history-of-public-spending-borrowing-and-debt-in-independent-ireland/.

Hoffman, Bryce. 2018. "If You Aren't Worried about a Trade War, You Don't Know about the Chicken Tax." *Forbes*, March 5. https://www.forbes.com/sites/brycehoffman/2018/03/03/if-you-arent-worried-about-a-trade-war-you-dont-know-about-the-chicken-tax/#1c74578d5455.

Koh, Eun Lee. 2000. "Following Up; Time's Hands Go Back on National Debt Clock." *New York Times*, August 13. https://www.nytimes.com/2000/08/13/nyregion/following-up-time-s-hands-go-back-on-national-debt-clock.html.

Lahart, Justin. 2007. "In Time of Tumult, Obscure Economist Gains Currency." *Wall Street Journal*, August 18. https://www.wsj.com/articles/ SB118736585456901047.

McMahon, Fred. 2016. "History Is Clear—High Tariffs and Trade Wars Devastate Countries." *Fraser Institute Blog*, October 3. https://www. fraserinstitute.org/blogs/history-is-clear-high-tariffs-and-trade-wars-devastate-countries.

Minsky, Hyman. 1974. "The Fragile Financial System." *New York Times*, August 31. https://www.nytimes.com/1974/08/31/archives/the-fragile-financial-system.html.

Nkusu, Mwanza. 2013. "Boosting Competitiveness to Grow out of Debt: Can Ireland Find a Way Back to Its Future?" IMF Working Paper No. 13/35, International Monetary Fund, February 1. https://www.imf.org/ en/Publications/WP/Issues/2016/12/31/Boosting-Competitiveness-to-Grow-Out-of-Debt-Can-Ireland-Find-a-Way-Back-to-Its-Future-40291.

Reuters. 2017. "China Central Bank Warns against 'Minsky Moment' Due to Excessive Optimism." October 18. https://www.reuters.com/article/ us-china-congress-debt-minskymoment/china-central-bank-warns-against-minsky-moment-due-to-excessive-optimism-idUSKBN1CO0D6.

Made in the USA
Coppell, TX
11 January 2020